Taking It to

Our Knees

Declaring Who I Am

Craig D. Lounsbrough

Beacon Publishing Group
ISBN (Paperback): 9781961504189
ISBN (Hardback): 9781961504196

Cover Design by Lori Pace
Interior Design by Lori Pace
Edited by Bobby Collins

Beacon Publishing Group, New York, NY 10001
www.beaconpublishinggroup.com

Manufactured in the United States of America

Additional Books by Craig D. Lounsbrough
with Beacon Publishing Group

Licensed Professional Counselor,
Certified Professional Life Coach,
Ordained Minister, Published Author

Join Craig at:

▶ YouTube @craiglounsbrough
www.facebook.com/craiglpc
www.linkedin.com/in/craiglpc/
www.craiglpc.com

Dedication

"I am currently engrossed in a very inspiring book that a great friend of mine recently gave me. I think it might be his best work. I was particularly mesmerized as I was reading the back jacket, and the book opened to page 179. I read the prayer, and it really hit home. My, how God works, and His timing is perfect."

The 'friend' was me. The book was my previous release. The book jacket simply talked about prayer. And as for page 179, God knows what we're going to write before we ever write it, and what someone else needs to "I am read before they ever read it. It is a choreographing of the most ingeniously divine sort. And for one man who picked up this book, page 179 was one of those moments.

I had written two dedications prior to this one, being satisfied with neither. I had revised both repeatedly, with each revision somehow moving me further away from whatever it was that I was seeking. While the rest of the book largely flowed (expect for those moments when it did not), somehow the dedication eluded me at ever greater distances.

After six months of vigorous writing, I had completed this book several weeks before I got the text from John. However, the dedication had continued to elude me.

I had traveled back to my childhood home in Ohio to enjoy a week away from the incessant and wearying demands of the counseling office. I had journeyed back to the home where I was born in order to evaluate how I had lived so that I might better determine the manner in which

I should someday die. In these latter years, was I on track? Were the dreams that had so captivated me and driven me of God, or were they of myself? Was this the way in which God would have me round out this journey? I was vexed with the questions.

And part of these questions involved another important question. Do I lay down the demands of writing and let what I have written to date be the conclusion of my words to the world? Have I said enough? After over twenty years of writing, do I step away from sentence, syntax, verb, and vowel? Is the writing concluded, or possibly is it exhausted? And then sitting in a restaurant the text came.

A single page touched a man's life. A handful of words aimed themselves at the bullseye of a soul worn and weary. Sentence and syntax, verb, and vowel met a man in a desperate place and made that place a bit less desperate. And on a Tuesday evening at 7:36 p.m. John sent a text about the impact of page 179 on his life.

Many others had commented about other pages and what those pages had done for them. But John was different. John was a lifelong friend. A fellow traveler of over six decades. Someone's who journey had its share of disappointment, setbacks, betrayal, grief, physical complications, and painful loss.

And in reading the text it came to me that if I can somehow take a handful of words (despite how much time and energy it might take to form them) and hit the bullseye of a soul worn and weary, I am convinced that I need to continue to do that. There are many John's out. One John who I know, but many Johns that I will never meet. And if

I can do something that touches people such as these, I feel compelled by God to do so. That is how I wish to live in order to prepare to die.

And therefore, the pages ahead are written out of the hope that one of them will hit the bullseye of your soul. It doesn't matter if one page does that for you, or if many are able to do that. As long as one does, I will continue to keep writing them in sentence, syntax, verb, and vowel. I will pen pages that touch souls.

Therefore, this book is committed to all who find a page or two hitting the bullseye of your soul. Whoever you are, these pages are written for you. I will likely never know you, but that doesn't mean that I can't encourage. And therefore, these pages are penned for you. May God use them in a choreography of the most ingeniously divine sort.

Taking It to Our Knees

Declaring Who I Am

Table of Contents

Introduction

"Who am I?" How many times have we circled back to that question? How many times has life shaken us to the point that we find ourselves wondering if we are who we thought we were? How often has our most recently fabricated identity collapsed under our latest setback and we find ourselves standing at some place in our lives asking the same question all over again? A friend confronts us. Our review went horribly bad. A spouse leaves. An investment imploded. The genius of our idea turned out to be anything but genius. And the question resurfaces. "Who am I?" How many times have we circled back to that question?

We've circled back to it because we've never gotten the answer. And we've never gotten it because the answer doesn't lay in any of the places that we've gone searching for it. We're looking for the answer to one life's biggest questions in all of the places where it will never be found.

We're seeking out an identity that will mesh well with our jobs, or please our families, or align with the culture, or comfortably fit in our social group, or grant our lagging sense of self-confidence a desperately needed boost. And in order to mesh, and please, and align, and fit, and grant us something that we're desperate for we're tried on a bunch of ill-fitting identities. We've pushed, and pressed, and literally pried ourselves into a ragtag collection of ill-fitting identities in this desperate effort to fit in.

And in all the tussling and struggling and force-fitting we find ourselves standing amidst piles of discarded identities that never did what we thought they would do. And now the question is louder than ever. "Who am I?" This whole misdirected effort is something akin to spending the whole of our lives in a fitting room full of clothes that never fit because we're embarrassed by the ones that do, or we're jealous of the ones that won't.

Who You Are Not

Who you are is not something that you try on. It's something that you are. It's not something that people dictate. It's something that God designed. It's not based on circumstance. It grows because of circumstance. It's not something that bows to the demands of the culture. It's something that seeks to transform the culture. Who you are is not the byproduct of some indiscriminate collection of painful deficits, dark histories, shifting cultural criteria, family dynamics, relational losses, or deflated self-esteem.

Your identity is a methodically rogue, wildly ingenious, entirely purposeful, and eternally irreplaceable design whose attributes were expressly created to be unleashed into the time in history within which you have been strategically placed. Indeed, your identity is greater than all of the things that would seek to shape it, crush it, define it, describe it, control it, or somehow deter it.

Who You Are Answered

So…"Who are we?" God has already told us. Plainly. And He did so because He knew that we would fall easy prey to an indiscriminate collection of painful deficits, dark histories, shifting cultural criteria, family dynamics, relational losses, or deflated self-esteems. He knew that our jobs, our families, the culture, our social groups, and our lagging sense of self-confidence would send us running on wild errands in an effort to discover an identity that would somehow meet all of their combined demands or offset their painful messages.

And God knew that if we fell to such things as these, we would forever forfeit the genius of the one-of-a-kind design that will never be replicated in the life of any other human being. He knew that a life of fitting rooms would leave us with a mountain of discarded identities. And He knew that those discarded identities would do nothing other than perpetuate a question that would only grow louder with each identity that we tried on. "Who am I?"

Thirty-One Declarations

This devotional outlines thirty-one Biblical declarations that embody the essence of who you are. Thirty-one things that declare your true identity. Your God-given identity. Your forever identity. Thirty-one truths that stand against the messages delivered by every painful deficit, the darkness of your history, the shifting cultural criteria that threatens to sideline you, the family dynamics that have alienated you, and the deflated self-esteem that has lied to you. Thirty-one truths that stand against everything that is not standing for you.

This book was written to help you find 'you.' Not some idealized self. Not some cheap forgery or shallow compromise. Not the self-that's run after the acceptance of people who will never give it to you, or the self-that's running from those messages. But the 'you' that God declares you to be. The eternal you. The unshakable you. May the next thirty-one days introduce you to a 'you' that is more than you could have possibly imagined, deeper than you thought feasible, greater than any success or combination of successes, and exceeding all of the combined accolades of mankind.

The Structure of This Book

This book is broken into two sections. Section One address five common areas of our lives that have a negative impact on our identity. These areas tend to skew or altogether suffocate our true identity, thereby leaving us to live out a less than vibrantly authentic life. These specific areas are outlined as a means of developing a foundation that will enhance the Thirty-One day experience for the reader.

Section Two draws directly from the Thirty-One "I Am" statements found in the Bible. These represent God's indisputable declaration of who you are. Each day elaborates on a particular "I Am" statement. This allows the reader to immerse themselves in each individual statement in order to maximize the impact of each statement on their lives, their relationships, their hopes, their dreams, and their futures.

Welcome to you!

Section One

Chapter One

Defined by Our Deficits

"*Any deficit that you have can never stand against the asset that that deficit is waiting to become.*"

~ Craig D. Lounsbrough

We come to define ourselves more by what we lack than by what we possess. We define ourselves by the successes that we haven't had, the relationships that didn't work, the careers that never happened, and the dreams that never got off the ground because they never made it to the runway.

All of these things tell us everything that we are not. The assets that we don't have. The confidence that we lack. The intelligence that is never intelligent enough. The talents that we don't possess, and the determination that is never sufficiently determined. We see ourselves as a sad compilation of everything that we are not.

These deficits result in shattered relationships. Shuttered opportunities. Job losses. Financial failures. Addictions. Upended careers. Friendships that went up in flames and the charred remains of families that fell to the same fate. Every failure. Every disappointment. Every loss. The shame and embarrassment mocks us, telling us that we are everything that is wrong with everything that went wrong.

Surrounded by so many failures that evidence both the depth and number of our deficits, we become defined by those deficits. We feel that there is nothing else that we can define ourselves by. The overwhelming preponderance of our failures, and disappointments, and losses, and failed dreams

11

obliterates anything other than the deficits to which all of these things speak. We can see nothing else, so we come to believe that there is nothing else. We are lulled (or sometimes thrust) into the belief that we are the sum total of our failures. And soon, believing becomes becoming.

The Power of Thought

Proverbs 23:7 says, "For as he thinks in his heart, so is he…" That's both incredibly powerful, but wildly dangerous. We become what we think. Our thinking possesses the power to shape our humanity, whether that shaping is accurate or not. We think ourselves into who we are.

Therefore, we can think ourselves into the deficits that we think about. We can let those things define us until we ourselves are convinced of that definition. Broken relationships. Job losses. Financial failures. Addictions. Dreams that die. Upended careers. Friendships and families that went up in flames. These become the essence of 'us,' and we become the reality of them. They singlehandedly define who we are.

The Question…

The question then becomes, "Who are we really?" Are we defined by our deficits? Is that our lot in life? Is there no escaping the things that we've screwed up?

Do they leave an indelible mark of defeat and incompetence?

Our Greatest Assets in Disguise

Or, are our deficits are greatest assets in disguise? Is it possible that we are defined far more by the potential that rests in the deficit than the deficit itself? Do the roots of something great lie deep in our worst failures?

Our lives are assets in the making. We are always standing on the verge of becoming something better. Something greater. The 'better' in our lives is always just one step away. One decision away. One choice away. On attitude shift away. The 'better' is always that close and never any farther away despite the deficits that seem intent on cannibalizing any asset that we might have.

The asset that any one of our deficits can become will always be far greater than the deficit from which it arose. Assets birthed of our deficits become the greatest parts of who we are. Taking what we believe to be defeat, seeing the rudimentary elements of victory embedded in that defeat, and turning that defeat into decisive victory is the stuff of true victory. Life-altering victory. Liberating victory. Transformational victory. But most importantly, achievable victory.

It's All Backwards

God turns life on its head. He reverses the order of things. What is dead dies to death and becomes alive. Water surrenders its fluidity to feet that tread on it. Blindness becomes blinded by light. Legs that limp become legs that leap. Food for thousands from food for one. Millions from pennies. It's all backwards. Gloriously backwards.

Sin destroys. It sets everything back. That's its single mission and sole agenda. God not only shuts sin down, He throw it in reverse. He works it against itself. As Joseph said to his brothers, "You intended to harm me, but God intended it for good..." It's all reversed. God walks us back from death to life. From hopelessness to hope. From fear to faith. From lives engulfed in deficits to lives empowered by assets.

We Don't Think That Way

The problem is, we don't think that way. Any belief that things might actually work this way is beaten out of us by the messages that our failures have beaten into us. We might visualize stopping something bad in our lives, or at least slowing it down. Maybe we can reign it in or temper it a bit. We might be able to draw some energy out of it so it's not quite as destructive, or maybe we can take some wind out of its sails.

But we don't think in terms of reversals. Radical, impossible, improbable, ingenious, and wildly liberating reversals. Sin says that we can't do that. God says that we're supposed to do that. We're not bold enough to think that way, but God naturally functions that way.

The Purpose of Deficits

Our deficits were meant to be reversed. Entirely. That's what we have them for. And in the reversal they become the assets that we never visualized them becoming. Deficits are the perfect seedbed for the birth and cultivation of stunning abilities. Hidden within our failures there lays all of the composite parts that set the stage for our greatest successes. The worst of us contains the lessons that teach us how to be the best of us.

Therefore, our deficits do not define who we are. Rather, they tell us who we can become. They are the worst of us waiting to become the best of us. They are the things that God is waiting to throw into reverse.

You Are More…

The deficits that define you are the ones that you've allowed to define you. God says that you are more than any deficit or combination of deficits. And that 'more' is boldly and unashamedly outlined in the thirty-one days of prayer that follow. That 'more' is laid out for you to embrace, ingest, and incorporate into your life in wildly wonderful and transformational ways. Your 'more' is waiting for you in the pages that follow.

Notes:

_____

_____

_____

_____

_____

_____

_____

_____

_____

_____

_____

_____

_____

_____

_____

Section One

Chapter Two

Defined By History

"The nature of our histories are always secondary to what we choose to do with them."

~ Craig D. Lounsbrough

Our histories impact us. However, what impacts us doesn't define us. Our histories can scar us, cripple us, leave us plagued with deficits, and reeling from loss. Our histories can leave us with overwhelming insecurities, fears that sabotage our dreams, and a deeply running pessimism that runs rogue over anything that might appear to possess some bit of desperately needed hope. They can leave us with deep-seated trauma, an addiction that won't relent, an inability to develop meaningful relationships, and a haunting sense that the effects of our past will engulf the whole of our future.

Our histories might define our journey to this point, but they do not possess the power to dictate that journey from this point forward. They might tell the tale of where we've been, but they have no power to pave the road to where we're going. History ends at today, not at a tomorrow that's not here yet. History cannot step beyond this moment unless we give it permission to do so. Clearly, its effects go forward and the healing that we need might take time. But the nature and character of our histories can end here. Clearly, our histories impact us. However, what impacts us doesn't define us.

A New Thing

In Isaiah 43:19 God says, "See, I am doing a new thing! Now it springs up; do you not perceive it? I am making a way in the wilderness and streams in the wasteland."

The unashamed and radical boldness in this verse is both rich and raw. The past ends here. Decisively. Right here. In the 'now' of our existence. God draws a hard line that halts 'what was' and unleashes 'what will be.' He Who is timeless cuts time in two. The story of yesterday is stripped of the power to pen the script of tomorrow. All is new!

God states that He is "doing a new thing." Not some slick revision. Not an overhaul. Not something old dressed up to look like something new. Not some clever nip-and-tuck. He is doing a "new thing." Something revolutionary. Something that sheds the past. Something that peels away the insecurities, crushes the fear, rips away the pessimism, shakes us free of the trauma, and breaks the back of the addiction. God is the great insurrectionist, rising up against the past and crushing it in the rising.

Revolutionary

The tone of 'something new' in this verse suggests something unexpected. Something whose newness is so 'new' that it breaks the back of our logic and leaves our reasoning entirely out of breath. It's 'new' to the point that it catches us entirely off guard. It's not something 'new' that we might devise or cook up in our heads because there's typically not a whole lot of anything new in that kind of stuff.

Rather, it's something so wildly revolutionary and so far out-of-the-box that it will defy all of the shortsighted paradigms that we use to make sense of it. Its radicalness will refuse to be held hostage to the diminishment of our logic. The fact that it makes no sense is exactly what makes sense simply because the genius of God will always outflank the logic of men. God's kind of newness will always demand a radical revision of what we had conceptualized as new.

Not Our History

And God does this 'something new' because there is no need to be held hostage to our histories. That's not God's intent. That's not His design. The scars, the insecurities, the fears, the pessimism, the trauma, the addictions, the inability to develop meaningful relationships, and the haunting sense that our past will engulf the whole of our future are not who we are. Rather, they are the results of what happened to us.

These things might be how people have come to define us. A spouse, or a friend, or an employer, or a family member, or some random person functioning out of some thoughtless mindset might have slapped these definitions upon us once-upon-a-time. Someone might have looked for some handy way to conveniently define us in a manner that was comfortable for them, and so they cherry-picked some assorted bits of our history and declared us to be those things. And while our histories might hold a bunch of these kinds of people, we are none of what they have declared us to be.

Rather, our histories are what we have experienced. They are the roads that we walked, the scars that we carry, the memories that haunt us, the legacies left behind us, and the regrets that chase us. Yet, despite the power and place that all of these might hold in our lives, they cannot and will not define who we are. God says that they are bound to their time…for all time.

God is "doing a new thing." Not a continuation of what was. Not some cheap addendum. Not some hat-trick. But something new. This newness declares that we are not held hostage to the way in which the past has attempted to defined us. We are not sentenced to walk with some impermeable definition that has already determined the nature of our future as well as our role in that future. Life is never held a prisoner to what we've done or what was done to us. The ability to be different will always crush that which declares that we will never be different.

Building Blocks

Rather, your past holds the building blocks of your greatness. Your past holds the essential raw materials for the very things that God is determined to build you into. Your past is the resource for your future, not the story of your future. It is a massive storehouse of incalculable assets capable of constructing a fresh tomorrow. Our history is not what defines us. It's what enlarges us, enlivens us, empowers us, and thrusts us up and out of whatever yesterday was into everything that tomorrow can be. Your past is not who you are. Your past is the accumulation of untapped resources standing ready to be unleashed into your today and delivered into your every tomorrow.

More Than Your History

You are more than your history. No history, despite how massive can define a single human being. You are far more than the accumulation of years, experiences, disappointments, betrayals, losses, frustrations, and failures. The nature of your humanity is vast beyond a hundred lifetimes and a million experiences. You cannot be defined by your past. It's simply impossible. No one's past could ever hope to contain enough content to define the limitlessness of their humanity. Yet despite the frequently painful nature of your past, you can be enriched by it. That is what God seeks to do in your life. Behold, He is doing a new thing in you.

The thirty-one days that lies ahead will help to break you from your history. These thirty-one statements made by God Himself declare that you are bound to nothing other than the magnificence of your design. History is the recounting of what has passed, not the declaration of who you are. Your history contains the painful but precious assets that God uses to enhance that magnificence. Your history is at God's disposal and He is already in your future. And He wants you to know that you are more than both.

Notes:

_____

_____

_____

_____

_____

_____

_____

_____

_____

_____

_____

_____

_____

Section One

Chapter Three

Defined By Cultural Criteria

"When they ridicule me and tell me that my need to do the 'right thing' is embedded in an overweening insecurity about doing the 'wrong thing,' I quickly inform them of three things. First, I inform them that it is nothing of a need born of fear, but everything of a choice born of conviction. Second, that it is nothing of insecurity, but it is everything of a strength that is sturdy and amply sufficient to field the most caustic of criticisms cast against it. And third, that this strength is far more potent than the pathetic weakness out of which their criticisms arise."

~ Craig D. Lounsbrough

Rubrics and More Rubrics

The culture is full of rubrics. Cheaply crafted rubrics. These rubrics are defined by what is loosely determined to be vogue, trendy, politically correct, in lock-step with progressive thought, and anointed by whoever's doing the anointing at any particular time. These rubrics are always shifting, ill-defined, and possess a shelf-life that's about as short as the attention span of those who dreamt them up.

These rubrics are typically granted a sense of rightness and correctness without any evaluation as to either. They're viewed as defining the current state of societal evolution as it supposedly trends toward a more enlightened society. As such, the greater the radical nature of them the more the evidence that they are truly breaking away from a dying order and declaring the dawning of a fresh new culture.

These rubrics become the template by which groups and individuals are evaluated as to whether they are cooperating with this progressive evolution or whether they are not. If it is determined that they are not, they are assigned any number of derogatory labels. These are typically categorized into a variety of negative stereotypes that are held as defining the persons that they're labeling. Such labeling creates a handy categorization that can be used to diminish, marginalize, discredit, or exclude certain groups of people that are deemed as an obstruction to the evolving culture.

The Cost of Not Fitting In

Therefore, the cost of not 'fitting in' becomes incrementally greater the more that we deviate from the vogue, trendy, politically correct, progressive thought that's forced upon us. The greater our divergence the greater the cost.

This creates a dilemma of identity. Do we borrow the ever-shifting identity of the culture, or do we press the culture aside sufficiently enough to determine who we are as a unique individual existing within the larger culture? Do we heed the pressures to be what the larger culture demands us to be? Do we listen to the voices around us who constantly bombard us with their assessment of who we are? Do we allow any of the elements within our culture tell us who we are, such as our families, our communities, our jobs, the accepted cultural mantras, or the organizations to which we belong?

The demand for adherence is incessant, pressing, and coercive. The culture struggles knowing what to do with people who refuse to embrace the cultural narrative. Deviance is considered unsettling, inconvenient, ignorantly rogue, and obstructive. It doesn't mesh well, or it's considered blatantly adversarial. It's messy and irritating to those who are incessantly beating the drums of lesser cultural agendas. Therefore, the pressure to conform is intense. The demands for adherence are ruthless.

The more that we reject what our culture demands that we be, the more alienation we experience. We are subjected to punitive measures and pressed further and further outside the mainstream culture. At some point we're removed entirely, yet we remain battered, belittled, and criticized despite the fact that we've been exiled.

Who Will We Choose to Be?

The culture can't define you. It doesn't have that kind of power and it certainly doesn't possess any such privilege. People and organizations and the larger culture can say any number of things about you. They can criticize you, make declarations about you, label you in any number of ways, or stereotype you in order to force-fit you into their agendas or force-fit you right out of the culture.

Yet, you are none of these things. Criticisms, declarations, labels, and stereotypes are far too small to express the fullness of your humanity. These are weak definitions of something far too big to define. Yet if we bend to them, they leave us living out a pasty-thin identity that is a horrific exploitation of who we actually are.

Who We Are

No element of our culture can define you. No culture possesses the capacity to do that. No part of the culture has the depth to define the depth within us. The culture doesn't define us because it can't. The fact is, it can't even define itself.

We are defined by something far greater than the culture. Something that outlasts and outlives any culture. We are defined by the God Who created us. Nothing can define us except that which determined what our definition was to be. Nothing else understands the whole of us except that which created the whole of us. Nothing else understands the intricacies, the nuances, and the ingenuity of a design that lays leagues beyond the intellect of any man or collection of men.

Breaking Away

The culture has made many demands of us. Many messages have been sent to us. Many characterizations have been made. Labels have been assigned. Definitions have been plastered all over us. Traits ascribed and values determined. And all of this will continue.

Yet, none of these define you. None of them can. None of them ever had. Therefore, don't grant them power to do what they cannot. Yet, over time we have carried these definitions. And as we have carried them we begin to act on them. When we act on some belief we are likely to get results that mirror the belief upon which we acted. Therefore, if we act on the things that the culture has defined us as being, the results are likely to confirm that we are those things. We then embody them as the essence of our character and nature of our being.

Thirty-One Things God Says You Are

Yet, you are none of these. You can't be. You won't be. And you can't be because you are far too vast to be fully defined by any one of them or any assorted collection of them. Only God can define who you are. He's got the blueprint. The only thing that the culture's got is a few errant scribbles on an illegible scrap of paper that they can't find half the time.

This devotional is designed to highlight the thirty-one things that God says you are. This devotion stands against what the culture has said you are. And this book works against the cultural declarations by declaring who God says you are. It's time to listen to a higher authority. It's time to listen to the God Who created you. Only He knows you from the best of yourself to the worst of yourself. And this God is calling you to your authentic self. The adventure begins as we rip away the definitions that the culture has branded us with and trade those scarring declarations for the

31

pristine and glorious design that God has infused within us.

Notes:

_____

_____

_____

_____

_____

_____

_____

_____

_____

_____

_____

_____

_____

_____

_____

_____

_____

_____

Section One

Chapter Four

Defined by Self-Esteem

"I can only imagine how much low self-esteem has robbed us as individuals and ransacked our culture. It is a rogue beast bent on diminishing us to some point of forlorn incapacity. Plagued by this beast, we live out marginalized lives that surrender the accomplishments and forsake the achievements that could have been ours. We grope through this existence meagerly living out each day by surviving each day, rather than realizing that we can live with an intensity that will have caused the day to finish having survived us."

~ Craig D. Lounsbrough
From "The Self That I Long to Believe In"

We are not defined by the worst-case assessment of ourselves, although we tend to render just such an assessment. We hand-pick the worst of ourselves to define the whole of ourselves. We do that because the worst of ourselves always seems to render the best of ourselves less than whatever best it might actually be.

Our attitudes trend toward the downside of whoever it is that we are. The deficits. The failures. The reversals. The relationships that never happened or shouldn't have happened. The goals that fell to the things that got in the way. Dreams that were crushed under the heel of reality. Choices that turned sour. Careers that died at the hands of corporate wrangling. Opportunities squandered. Surrender to fear when we should have feared the idea of surrender. We trend toward our interpretation of what these things say about us.

The Application of Our Interpretations

Once we've developed these interpretations of ourselves we apply them liberally. Their repeated application creates a negative skew where everything is painted in undesirable and self-defeating tones. The best of us never escapes the interpretation of the worst of us. Some small and commonplace error becomes catastrophic. An inconsequential misstep evidences our unworthiness. The normal hit-and-miss of life is turned into a relentless barrage of not so friendly-fire where we cut ourselves to ribbons.

If there is anything that appears to be good in us we eye it with a penetrating suspicion. We must have missed something. The good must be an illusion based on our naivete. There has to be some sort of deceptive trickery in it all where we've fooled ourselves into believing in this apparent good. Sooner or later this thing will show itself to be the bad that it must be. That it has to be. And if the bad doesn't reveal itself, we will impregnant it with something that is certain to sabotage the good that we simply can't accept.

We wordsmith a plot that crafts a fictional 'bad' so compelling that we become thoroughly convinced of its existence. We will spin-a-tale to soundly refute the good and declare it as a fraudulent facsimile of something that it is not and will never be. We develop this self-deprecating dialogue that becomes the imaginary biography that touts the attributes of our stupidity, our immaturity, or our lackluster personality. We compile an unending catalog packed full of the deficits that render us as a non-entity in a world that's squandering its resources by charitably providing us some bit of space within it. We nurture this plummeting self-esteem until it disintegrates in atmosphere of our attitude.

Defined by a Fraudulent Identity

In time and over time we come to believe ourselves to be who and what we've told ourselves we are. We become convinced of our own self-deprecating narrative. The fictional account becomes the non-fiction of our existence. We find ourselves unable to entertain any other possible interpretation of who we are and who we can yet become. We cannot comprehend another story. A different tale. Some other biographical rendering.

An Authentic Script

We become locked in a story not our own. We play a role fabricated of a false self. We continually force ourselves into alignment with this story because we have come to believe that the 'force-fitting' is actually some sort of self-actualizing struggle.

Yet, in some deep place the heart yearns for a different script. A more authentic script. Something that has a tinge of truth to it that we find eerily compelling. The force-fitting has a bit of a disingenuous feel to it. Something got lost in the editing, but the threads of that 'something' remain traceable between the lines of our narratives. And our momentary glimpses of these things create a tentative bit of excitement that maybe we might be more.

We Are More

No narrative can capture the whole of who you are. And no narrative can destroy that either. The vastness of your humanity will always escape the scope of any words that we might use to either define it or hold it hostage. In the same vein, the narratives crafted by our deficits, our failures, the reversals, the relationships that failed, he goals that fell, the dreams that were crushed, the choices that turned sour, the careers that died, the opportunities that were squandered, our surrender to fear…none of these can craft a narrative even remotely capable of embodying the entirety of who we are.

You are vaster than everything that would seek to define you, even if the person that's doing the defining is you. In speaking to God, the Psalmist said, "I praise you because I am fearfully and wonderfully made…" That's your narrative. That's your story. That's who and what you are.

You aren't just one of many. You're not just another person walking around on a planet populated by eight billion other people who are just walking around as well. You are "fearfully and wonderfully made." Your design is the product of an infinite genius crafting a one-of-a-kind human being whose skill-sets and attributes were specifically fashioned to impact the point in history into which you were placed. That's your story. That will always be your story.

I would have you think about this. Read this carefully and slowly:

"Whatever you see within yourself, let it be
the whole of yourself. For too often we have been
brutalized by our own sense of inadequacy and we've
been held hostage to the lesser choices born of such a
debilitating sense of self. Know this, that latent within
you there lies more than ample resources begging to
be called forth to smash the chains forged of such an
incapacitating sense of self. And it is my prayer that
you would press against everything within you that
would hold you back, and that you would raise
whatever voice you have and extend that call."
~ *Craig D. Lounsbrough*
From "The Self That I Long to Believe In"

The thirty-one "I am" statements that follow will help you to understand "that latent within you there lies more than ample resources begging to be called forth to smash the chains forged of such an incapacitating sense of self." God writes the narrative, and that narrative is illustrated in the thirty-one days that follow. That narrative sets itself squarely against the low self-esteem that's been dogging you steps and darkening your days. It is my prayer that this book allows you to dramatically edit your lackluster narrative into God's glorious narrative.

Section One

Chapter Five

Defined by Our Physical Appearance

"If the mirror doesn't give me much back,
it's because it's not designed to reflect the
things within me that make the reflection
truly magnificent."

~ Craig D. Lounsbrough

The world has set an airbrushed standard of what we're supposed to look like. This photoshopped menagerie of idealized versions of a perfected humanity demands something of us that none of us can achieve. Even those whose images are altered to this definition of perfection are themselves nothing of the sort.

The culture defines beauty but it cannot demonstrate what they define as beauty unless they fabricate it. Physical perfection is the illusion that eludes anyone who claims it or pursues it. It's the design of people who themselves cannot achieve the design that they both create and propagate. This perfection is declared as some pinnacle whose pursuit is the holy grail of our existence. It is decreed as the key that opens doors that will never open for the less desirable. It will elicit favors that the more homely among us can never elicit. In essence, its value is non-negotiable.

Misappropriated Investments

Therefore, we rigorously invest in a host of surgeries, a variety of cutting-edge procedures, and an assorted collection of creams and lotions. We sweat through an endless variety of trendy workouts that claim to put us one step closer to this pinnacle of our humanity. We dive into whatever diet that happens to have the blessing of some trending celebrity or health guru. We spend hours preening in front of the mirror. We take thousands of selfies in order to capture just the right angle that accentuates everything that we want to accentuate, and that hides everything that we don't.

Our interactions with the world around us becomes dictated by a shrewd and entirely exhausting game of flaunting that which we believe to be beautiful and disguising that which we don't. We are driven to present a pristine self that is pressed, clean, orderly, well-groomed, tight in the right places, and loose in the places that enhance our appearance. We have a checklist of grooming dos and don'ts that we run through before we step out of whatever door we're about ready to step out of.

The Priority of Our Appearance

Imagine, if you will, the amount of energy that we invest in our appearance. Imagine the amount of time, money, and personal resources that we squander on what we look like. And with such a grossly disproportionate investment in the external, the internal goes wanting. The essential essence of who we are is left languishing as the red-haired step-child to the physical part of ourselves that can never and will never define the whole of ourselves. We are ambushed by the power of the airbrush

The Vulnerability of the Veneer

Your humanity is too vast to be held hostage to the veneer of your appearance. The essence that you bring to your world is housed in the powerhouse of your humanity, not the smoothness of your complexion. Your abilities will always outclass your body type. Flexing a muscle changes nothing. Flexing your mind can change everything.

The veneers are a pathetic representation of what we think will garner the affection and attention of a world from which we seek acceptance at the sacrifice of self. Veneers are a mortifying trade-off where our desperate need for acceptance drives us to betray ourselves in a deathly exchange of identity for acceptance.

Defining Ourselves by Our Appearance

Despite its destructive nature, this photoshopped menagerie of idealized versions of a perfected humanity reigns over a deluded culture. It is the template by which all other templates are judged, modified or mortified. It is the reflection demanded of every mirror.

Acquiescing to this weak standard, we begin to judge ourselves in relation to that standard. We lay out some sort of culturally-biased continuum in our heads and then we gauge our value based on where we place ourselves on that continuum. We live a life where the entirety of our resources are spent fighting our way up that continuum. The understanding of who we are and any value that we possess becomes based on where we've landed on that continuum and how aggressively we're working our way up it (or have fallen down it).

In the book, "The Self that I Long to Believe In," I wrote the following: "Our existence alone is the greatest statement of our worth and the clearest evidence as to our value. What we do with that existence is up to us. But the sheer reality of that existence evidences value. The fact I am writing this and you are reading this attests to the fact that we both have immense value because we both exist to do both of those things."

That thought is built upon by a later quote in the book which reads: "Each of us needs to embrace the fact that our value is in who we are. And we need to widen that thought by understanding that this value that we carry within us exceeds our greatest estimation of it. It will readily eclipse anything that we do."

None of this has anything to do with our appearance. The essence of your greatness is not based on what you look like in any mirror. It's based on what you want to do with the person that's in the mirror. It's ferreting out the rich storehouse of gifts, talents, and abilities that reside within the heart. These will handily eclipse any reflection.

I would go so far as to say that cultivating who you are will lend such a power and vibrancy to your presentation that your physical appearance will be swallowed up in release of who you are. People won't seek you out because of how you look. They will seek out because you radiate something that swallows up the superficiality of what they've spent their lives pursuing.

You will exude something that their pursuit of beauty never gave them. The mirror will never reflect back to them what all of these things said it would reflect. And in time, they're going to come to you seeking out whatever you're exuding simply because their thirst for it has been repeatedly disappointed by all other things that they've invested themselves in. They will want what you have become.

The Reflection of Your Soul, Not Your Face

The devotional section that is to follow outlines thirty-one "I am" statements that God has made regarding who you are. These are the reflections that have value. These are the reflections that grant our lives the power and sense of satisfaction that no other reflection will be able to deliver. These are the things of real, lasting, transformational beauty.

Indeed, they are what's truly beautiful. They are elegant. Their beauty deepens with age and their power multiplies with time. Your appearance is enhanced to the point that no mirror can contain it or reflect it. That is what the following "I am" statements will deliver into your life, today and every day.

Notes:

_____

_____

_____

_____

_____

_____

_____

_____

_____

_____

_____

_____

_____

_____

_____

_____

_____

_____

Section One

Chapter Six

Defined by a Journey Gone Wrong

"To let myself be defined by my greatest mistakes is my greatest mistake."
~ Craig D. Lounsbrough

Craig D. Lounsbrough

It seems that we have some vague and rather ethereal sense of where we're going in this thing called life. For the more contemplative soul, that sense might be quite refined. For the casual traveler, it might be a bit more nebulous and scattered. In many cases where we're going is far more rigorously defined by all the places where we don't want to go, rather than the places where we do want to go. At other times, its definition is rather handily shaped by the opinions of others, or it's carved directly from the bedrock of the value systems that have been built into our lives throughout the whole of our lives. Vague or refined, we all have some sense of where we're going. And too often, we find ourselves ending up someplace else.

Some of us are not necessarily in conscious pursuit of wherever this place is. We have this instinctually primal sense that it's there and we intuitively assume that our path with take a natural course to wherever that place is. Then, there are others of us who are myopically focused on where we're going to the degree that everything that we do is wholly defined by that singularly beguiling destination. Some of the more adventurous souls among us nimbly pursue that destination, spiritedly pulling in as much of everything that we can along the way to accentuate both the journey as well as the destination. In whatever way we do it, we all have some sense of where we're going. And too often, we find ourselves ending up someplace else.

50

The Detours We Create

Yet, life is not so predictable as to always wind its way to the places that we presumed it to be going. There are those times when where we were going was bafflingly mistaken as some sort of final destination when in reality it was only a step to a final destination. At other times, the place where we're going is really a destination that we had fabricated because the place to which life had originally called us appeared too big, or too far, or too steep, or simply impossible in whatever way our limited vision happened to interpret it. At such times we craft some other less intimidating and thoroughly unfulfilling destination. And then in the magic of life, there are those times where we have pursued some authentic destination with such rigorous tenacity that the trajectory of our efforts have catapulted us past our destination to places that are everything of our furthest and fondest imagination. However it might play out, we're all headed somewhere.

The Detours Life Creates

But then there are those other times when life takes a sharp turn that seems little of our actions, nothing of our destination, but everything of circumstances designed to kill our journey and crush our destination long before we get within arm's length of it. There's a sense that something intrinsically unjust, stealthy and evil is always about and on the prowl, and whatever it is, it's bound to show up. When it does, it undoes everything that we thought was secure and certain, wreaking havoc on whatever our journey had been to that point. And to whatever degree it wrecks the road underneath our feet, we're left in a blurring trauma that renders our journey disjointed, our destination uncertain, and our lives dispirited.

Yet, more often than not it's the not the obvious shifts in our journey that are the core problem. Sure, life shows up and we get shoved down. There's no question that the natural ebb and flow of life, whether it be titanic or miniscule, will happen to us. Despite our frequently ego-centric inclinations to the contrary, we are not so shrewd or ingenious as to be able to traverse life in a manner that deftly side-steps everything that comes at us. We don't dance as well as we think we do. And so life will fall upon us, or ram against us, or pull the ground out from under us.

Casual and Careless

Yet, more often than not, the explanation doesn't rest in life having shown up. The much more poignant issue is that too often we are passive, flabby, and lax in rigorously living out our lives. We're far too casual and careless. Somehow, somewhere the exquisite sanctity of life and the priceless privilege of living it out was supplanted with some sense that it's too much work or that it's not going to work, so why try? The gift is lost in the grind and we lose a sustaining sense of gratitude. And so, we drift without knowing that we're drifting because we're no longer paying attention. The outcome of such passive living is that we end up finding ourselves somewhere else without ever seeing it coming.

Preoccupied with Pabulum

Too often we're too preoccupied with pabulum. We're tediously engaged with tiny things and we're caught in the tedium of minutia because we can gather these things around us and control them when the bigger things are out of our control. Too frequently we're goaded by the fear of big dreams and massive possibilities, so we dumb down our lives to anesthetize those fears. We're caught in small things, and the outcome is that we end up finding ourselves somewhere else without ever seeing it coming.

Along for the Ride

Frequently we presume that we're some docile passenger along for a ride that's going wherever it's going, so we just let it go to wherever that place is. We freely surrender to passivity which is an invitation to blindness. We then turn to the hovel of our small agendas because it's the only place that we now have to go. We become so entangled in the pull of our own flimsy agendas that we serve agendas that serve no other purpose than serving our agendas. Assuming we're on a ride that we can't direct, the outcome is that we end up finding ourselves somewhere else without ever seeing it coming.

The Walls of Denial

At other times, we live in the constructed confines erected from the raw material of denial, causing us to live out a life that is in denial of life itself. We become squatters living in a squatter's camp constructed by the flimsy materials of justification, rationalization, blame-placing and projecting. We pull in the walls due to the reality that materials of this sort are always pulling inward because they will die if we dare to press them outward. Hemmed in by walls of this sort, the world around us is shut out and moves on without our awareness of it. The outcome is that we end up finding ourselves somewhere else without ever seeing it coming.

Ending Up Somewhere

We will end up somewhere. The fact that we have a destination is irrefutable as life is a journey that presents us with no option other than the journey. We may decide that the nature and course of the journey is irrelevant and we may take a backseat to passivity. If we do, we have no right to complain when we end up in some place other than what we may have thought or preferred. However it happens, we will end up somewhere.

Defined by a Journey Gone Wrong

To whatever degree we have done it, we have contributed to where we find ourselves at this moment. The causations may have been largely of our making. Our poor decisions and impulsive choices may have landed us in dark places. We may have believed in the wrong things and justified those beliefs in spite of the painful outcomes that they repeatedly laid at our feet. We may have thought wrong, thought selfishly, abandoned any forethought, or not thought at all. Therefore, we thought ourselves to where we never thought we would be.

We may well be the author of our destinations and the surveyor of the roads that brought us to these places. Those places might be barren. They may be empty of everything for which we had hoped and void of the slightest piece of our slightest dreams. We may see no way out of them and therefore assume that we will be forced to surrender the rest of our lives journeying further into them.

All of this may be true. But what is truer is that you are not your destination. Your lack of judgement at a crucial crossroads may have placed you here, but you are more than the place at which you have arrived. Bad choices and even worse passions may have landed you in the wasteland that you're living in. But you are not what you see around you. You are not the place within which you have put yourself.

You are more than the choices that you made and the beliefs that you errantly embraced. You are more. And because you are, the place you are at is not the place where your will are doomed to live. You are more than what surrounds you and so is your future.

Notes:

_____

_____

_____

_____

_____

_____

_____

_____

_____

_____

_____

_____

_____

_____

_____

_____

_____

_____

_____

_____

Section One

Conclusion

"The safe story is the one that tells a tale
of who I am not, for that is a story that will
never demand the excellence for which I was born
and without which I will never really live."
~ Craig D. Lounsbrough

Who I am not!

A Declaration:

1. I will not condemn the essence of who I am in order to receive the accolades of who the world wants me to be.

2. I will not allow my identity to be edited into oblivion in order to be a line-item in someone's agenda.

3. I will not embrace the 'narratives of convenience' that others would have me live out for their ease and comfort.

4. I will not run from the magnificence of my design out of the fear of who and what I might actually be able to become.

5. I will not abandon the horizons for which I was created for in order to be a squatter in the box that the world has deemed as tidy and convenient.

6. I will not trade my God-given ingenuity for the squalor of obedience so as not to draw the ire of an insecure world.

What I am not!

A Dedication:

1. I am not the compilation of any deficits real or imagined, as assets born of our deficits become the most powerful part of who we ever hope to be.

2. I am not the accumulation of any historical record regardless of how sordid or glorious it might be, for history is rich with the assets that

will make tomorrow's history far greater than yesterday's.

3. I am not someone whose identity is determined by the rubrics that the world would force me into, for the expanse of my humanity is massive enough to be the rubric of the rubrics.

4. I am not the narrative written by others who confiscated my story in order to force it into the service of their agendas, for my story is too big to be forced into the smallness of any agenda.

5. I am not the summation of my failures, for my failures are the lessons upon which my successes are coming to completion.

6. I am not defined by the face in the mirror nor the criteria that the world would force on that face. Rather, I am defined by that which no mirror ever devised by man can reflect.

Notes:

_____

_____

_____

_____

_____

_____

_____

_____

_____

_____

_____

_____

_____

_____

_____

_____

_____

_____

_____

_____

_____

Section 2

31 Days of

Prayer

Day 1

I Am Adopted into God's Family

"…to redeem those under the law, that we might receive adoption to sonship. Because you are his sons, God sent the Spirit of his Son into our hearts, the Spirit who calls out, 'Abba, Father.' So you are no longer a slave, but God's child; and since you are his child, God has made you also an heir."
~ Galatians 4:5-7

Abandonment is commitment thrown into reverse. It's a promise repealed. A vow cancelled. A partnership revoked. It runs entirely against everything that makes us human. It is the recklessness of greed on a self-serving rampage.

Such actions render the idea of committed relationships as the stuff of disappointed fiction. Forever promises become the mirage of gullible heart's misled by the idealistic promises of love. We feel ourselves to be the fool exposed. Our value is obliterated. And we are left abandoned as castaways on some deserted island of tortured humanity, wondering if it would be wiser to simply remain in this barren place rather than risk leaving it only to have abandonment exile us here yet again.

Yet God's commitment know no reverse. His promises are never repealed. His vows hold tight for eternity. His partnership is unfailing. God knows no islands. With a steeled intent He said, "Never will I leave you; never will I forsake you." Out of that very promise God fashioned a commitment woven of a bond that is irreparable, invulnerable, and entirely invincible. His commitment is fashioned of things eternal and untouchable. God wishes to adopt you. To make you His own. To claim you outright. To put His indelible stamp on you and call you His forever child. And His adoption of us renders abandonment forever abandoned.

"The need to belong runs a course
directly through the apex of our soul. To know with
irrefutable certainty that others deem us as possessing
a value so indisputable that they would set the whole
of themselves aside in order to protect the whole of
ourselves. Without this to rest in there is no rest."
~ *Craig D. Lounsbrough*

Morning Prayer

Dear God:
I come to you alone this morning, when being alone is
the last thing that I want to feel and the last place that I
want to be. I feel like I'm a prisoner of the choices made
by someone else. I feel as if I have been exiled to some
horrible place where people are left alone and isolated
to deal with a pain that is so deep that they can't think
their way out of it.

I don't believe that relationships were meant to be
betrayed by abandonment. I don't believe that You
designed it that way. But it happens anyway. And while
I'd like to believe that these kinds of things always
happen to someone else, it happened to me. And so here
I sit, alone, isolated, and wishing that this were all a
dream.

Dear God, You have adopted me. You have made me
Your own. You have claimed me outright. You have
put Your indelible stamp on me and You call me Your
forever child. A thousand people can abandon me, but
all of these truths remain untouched. I embrace Your

adoption of me. I am Your own, and You are mine. Today and forever.

I pray all of this in Jesus's Name. Amen

A Thought to Carry with Me Today

"I may find myself discarded as rubbish along this road that we call life, having been left there by people who deemed my life as deficient and my humanity as expendable. But laying along that roadside awash in my own tears, I must remember that man's rubbish will never cease to be God's treasure."
~ *Craig D. Lounsbrough*

Before this day, I release to God...

_____

_____

_____

_____

_____

_____

Evening Prayer

Dear God:
As this day closes, I go to bed alone…but not. You are here with a fullness and intensity that surpasses any

Craig D. Lounsbrough

person or group of people I could be with right now. Your presence is all-encompassing. You are around me and within me. You sit right next to me while inhabiting the furthest corners of my mind all at the same time. You hold my every emotion in Your hands. You tend to my soul, healing it when it needs healing and calming it when it becomes anxious. You walk before me and behind me, never leaving your post even for the briefest second.

You have adopted every part of my being. Everything that I am is Yours, and You are everything that I need. Thank you for such a wonderful and enduring relationship.

I pray all of this in Jesus' Name. Amen.

A Thought to Prepare for Tomorrow
"God is already in the tomorrow that you are yet to show up for."
~ Craig D. Lounsbrough

From this day, I release to God...

_____

_____

_____

_____

_____

_____

Day 2

I Am a Child to the King of Kings

" Yet to all who did receive him, to those
who believed in his name, he gave the
right to become children of God—."
~ John 1:12

We want to be someone's child. To know where we came from. To know that those people and that place holds us with an impassioned and unbreakable love, even once we've moved on with our own lives or they have moved on with theirs. To know that this long lineage of people have funneled the essence of their existence into ours.

We want to belong to a lineage that is bigger than us and that grounds us in something beyond the limitations of our own finite existence. Where we've come from grants us a desperately needed identity. It enhances our sense of where we've going, how to better get there, and that we're not alone in the 'getting.' It tells us that we're part of a larger story and that we have been granted the immense privilege of enriching and perpetuating that story. It makes sense of the living and the dying that too often becomes the confining measures by which we define the whole of our lives and the extent of this existence.

We want to be someone's child. To be owned by the connection of blood, genetics, shared experiences, and the relationships drawn tight by those experiences. To share a joint lineage of generations past and a shared vision for the generations that are coming. Such a need is deeply engrained and eternally woven within the core of our humanity.

Paul said, "The Spirit himself testifies with our spirit that we are God's children." There is no greater affirmation. No greater declaration of Whose we are. Our earthly parents may have given us the whole of themselves, or they may have abandoned the whole of us in pursuit of themselves. Whatever our history, we want to be someone's child. To know where we came from. God is both and answers both.

"How astonishingly improbable that we
Could actually be children of the God of all creation.
But should such improbability actually be reality, how could we ever look in the mirror again without seeing something so utterly marvelous that we would be forced to spend the rest of our lives celebrating it?"
~ Craig D. Lounsbrough

Morning Prayer

Dear God:
I know that I will never outgrow the need to be someone's child. The days of childhood might pass, but the need to be a child never does. The farther that I venture out into the world, the more that I need the grounding of knowing that I am a part of someone else and that they are a part of me. In a world that alienates so many, knowing that this connection exists is priceless and entirely indispensable.

There are those who have those connections and are blessed because they do.

Then there are those who've found those connections severed, somehow fractured, or never having existed at all.

Yet, God we are all Your children. All of us. That is a connection impossible to sever, immune to fracture, and always having existed despite our frequent ignorance of it. I want to rest in that fact. I am Your child. I am Your sacred treasure. I am Your delight. I am loved with an intensity that I can't grasp. Today I call You "Abba Father."

I pray all of this in Jesus's Name. Amen

A Thought to Carry with Me Today
"I am descended from many things. Choices that I have made. Mistakes that still run hot on my heals. Marriages lost. Dreams abandoned. Friendships that failed. Children lost. And while I might be descended from these things, none of them birthed me."
~ *Craig D. Lounsbrough*

Before this day, I release to God...

_____

_____

_____

_____

Evening Prayer

Dear God:
Tonight, I ask you to tuck me in. Not in the sense of sheets and blankets. But tuck in my heart. My soul. My

mind. Tuck me in in such a way that I might sleep well tonight. But more than that, tuck me in in a manner that I might awaken with fear gone, anxiety eliminated, depression replaced with peace, anxiety with calm, and a sense that Your presence is everywhere.

Tuck me in as Your child. Tuck me in so that I wake to resentment dissipated, anger washed away, bitterness swept from my heart, and confidence restored. As Your child I come to You tonight asking You to be the Father that I know that You long to be. Heal Your child. Restore Your child. Love on Your child and teach this child to love on You.

I pray all of this in Jesus' Name. Amen.

A Thought to Prepare for Tomorrow
"God knows the day ahead, and what the day will be once it becomes the day behind. And He wants each one to great on both ends."
~ *Craig Lounsbrough*

From this day, I release to God...

_____

_____

_____

_____

_____

Day 3

I Am Passionately Loved

"You keep track of all my sorrows. You have
collected all my tears in your bottle. You have
recorded each one in your book."
~ Psalm 56:8

To be loved is to say that my humanity is valuable enough to be cherished by someone else. It is to say that in the busyness of a demanding world, I have a value this is not only recognized by someone else, but also significant enough that another person is actually compelled to act on that value. To be loved is to say that my existence as a single human being is worth being celebrated and cultivated by someone else who may get nothing out of that investment.

To be loved is to say that someone else sees enough value in me to take the limited resources that they have at their disposal and to direct those away from themselves and direct them into me. It is an incredibly endearing declaration. A deeply affirming acknowledgement. A confirmation that my existence matters.

Too often the world has forgotten to love. It's bent on chasing lesser things that enflame primitive passions and offer up short-term indulgences. The world is on mad rant of self-gratification where love has been redefined as some gluttonous endeavor. As such, love is often hard to find and even harder to give.

"For God so loved the world…." Yes, God loved the world…you and me. But in what way? In a way that moved God to sacrifice His Son so that we might be salvaged by that sacrifice. That's the kind of trade that love prompts, giving up the greater good of oneself for the greater good of another. To give us what we have no way of giving ourselves. To embrace the gloriously radical belief that any sacrifice that we might make is far better spent on another than on ourselves. And that is what God did…and does for you. Welcome to God's love!

"He said that the blood was not his own,
but that of a comrade a few feet away who had been blown apart by an enemy grenade. And after having left the rice paddies of Vietnam, he eventually took up residence in the pew of a small mid-western church. For he said that he had been covered by the blood of one friend in combat and by blood of another on a cross in another sort of combat. And such was his love for both that he committed to forget neither."
~ *Craig D. Lounsbrough*

Morning Prayer

Dear God:
Sometimes I'm afraid to be loved. I'm afraid to be loved and then find out that it wasn't love at all. Or to be loved and then to have that love taken away for reasons that had nothing to do with love. Or to be loved for what I could give to someone else, instead of being loved for the potential that I had to give to the world. It's risky to be loved.

But God, help me to let You love me. I mean a love beyond what I even understand or am capable of understanding on my own. Let me be loved by the kind of love that prompted You to send Your Son to His death for my life. That's a mind-boggling kind of love that I want to understand. I want to hold in my hands. I want to shelter in my heart. That's the kind of love that I want to wake up to and go to bed with every night.

The fact that You offer me that kind of love helps me to understand just how incredibly valuable I am to You. I want to rest in that, immerse myself in it, and live out every minute of my life absorbed in and by that kind of love.

I pray all of this in Jesus's Name. Amen

A Thought to Carry with Me Today
"How could we not be romantic, for the God
Who created us has never fallen out of love with us
despite all the many ways that we have
fallen out of love with Him."
~ Craig D. Lounsbrough

Before this day, I release to God...

_____

_____

_____

_____

_____

_____

_____

Evening Prayer

Dear God:

Love me to sleep tonight. Love me to sleep. That as I lay down my head I feel the warmth of Your love throughout the entirety of my being. Overwhelm me with Your love to the point that there is no shred of my life that is untouched by it. No shred. I cannot imagine a better way to sleep than to feel the power of that kind of love.

And when I awaken in the morning, awaken me with a sense of Your love to the degree that I am able to carry that throughout the day. No matter the difficulties. No matter how much stress I might face or how many problems might ram themselves into me. No matter how much misfortune life may throw at me, let me feel Your love. Thank you for seeing in me all of the things that would cause You to love me so much! I love you too.

I pray all of this in Jesus' Name. Amen.

A Thought to Prepare for Tomorrow

"The greatest gift in any gift is that there was someone who loved us so much that they simply could not keep themselves from giving the gift to us. And by far, the best example of that 'someone' is God. And the thing that He couldn't keep Himself from giving us was Himself."

~ *Craig D. Lounsbrough*

From this day, I release to God...

_____

_____

_____

_____

_____

_____

_____

Day 4

I Am a New Person

*"Therefore, if anyone is in Christ, the new creation
has come: The old is gone, the new is here!"*
~ 2 Corinthians 5:17

There are so many things about ourselves that we would love to get rid of. Things that we'd like to change, or memories that we'd like to burn out of our minds. We'd love to dump negative attitudes, generate some halfway decent belief in ourselves, crush an addiction that's crushing us, develop some sorely needed self-discipline, or shed the fear that keeps us hamstrung. The list seems long and unbearable.

And so we work to change these things, or get rid of them, or forget them altogether. We read stacks of self-help books. We go to counseling or find a life coach. We listen to endless podcasts, repeatedly commit to various programs, or craft a bunch of empty goals that we're constantly having to resurrect. Yes, we work to change these things.

But in the end, the kind of change that we're searching for remains elusive. We just can't get there. The kind of newness that we envision continually eludes our ability to bring it from vision to everyday reality. We just can't do it.

We are designed for more. But that 'something more' looms larger than our ability to achieve it. Yet in Christ, our limitations are smashed, our resources are fused with the infinite God, and we are made new simply by accepting Who He is and What He did for us. "I have been crucified with Christ. It is no longer I who live, but Christ who lives in me." With Christ embedded in us, our design is unleashed and everything that would diminish that design is undone. We are breathtakingly new!

"God has no interest in doing some slick Revisions or innovative tweaks in order to make transformation feel measured and safe. Rather, He's about delivering a sweeping overhaul to your life that will leave nothing untouched and everything transformed. Therefore, the question regarding transformation is whether we're brave enough to experience the transformation from which we cannot return but cannot miss."
~ *Craig D. Lounsbrough*

Morning Prayer

Dear God:
I want to be new. And I don't want that newness to be limited to my shallow understanding of newness, because my 'newness' is more about a bunch weak revisions versus a radical transformation. I don't want that. In fact, keep me from that.

I want You to make me new. Entirely new. Not just some convenient or piecemeal parts of who I am. Not just a handful of little things that gives the illusion that I'm really new. I don't want that. I want to be made radically and completely new in ways that I can't even envision. I want a liberating newness. A sweeping newness. Something that is so breathtakingly new that I won't even recognize who I am once You're done with me.

I give my life to You. I ask You to inhabit my soul, my heart, my mind, my every breath, and each thought that I will ever have. Come dear Lord Jesus and be 'Christ in me!' This is what I want because this is what will make me wildly and wonderfully new!

I pray all of this in Jesus's Name. Amen

A Thought to Carry with Me Today

"Let God define what newness is for you. For if you attempt to define it, you will stoop to sleepy revisions and superficial adjustments that will be no more 'new' than the 'old' that you thought you revised."
~ *Craig D. Lounsbrough*

Before this day, I release to God...

_____

_____

_____

_____

_____

_____

_____

_____

_____

Evening Prayer

Dear God:
Every day is a step in the process of becoming new. I'm not certain that the steps that I took today were large, or small, or something in-between. But what I do know is that the size of any step is always dwarfed by the fact that I took it. And I took some.

And so tonight I ask that whatever the steps were that I might have taken today that You would bless them. Make them great. Make them powerful. Make them transformational. Make them the next steps to the next thing. And then I would ask that You prepare me for the steps that are waiting for me tomorrow. Fill tomorrow, and every tomorrow after that with ever-increasing steps that result in an ever-increasing newness. Don't just live within me Jesus. Change me in the living. Transform me. Force the old out and press the new in. I submit myself to You tonight for every tomorrow that is to follow. Make me new.

I pray all of this in Jesus' Name. Amen.

A Thought to Prepare for Tomorrow
"Give God a little more time to do what you would screw up if you did it now."
~ Craig D. Lounsbrough

Taking It to Our Knees

From this day, I release to God...

_____

_____

_____

_____

_____

_____

_____

_____

Day 5

I Am Not Weary

"Come to me, all you who are weary and
burdened, and I will give you rest."
~ Matthew 11:28

Life seems to take more than it gives. There's an odd, almost fatal imbalance to it all. Our energies seem consumed by the everyday stuff, never mind anything additional that we might try to enjoy as some sort of reprieve. Just keeping pace is consuming.

But more so, living right demands even more energy. Making the right choices. Taking the high road. Standing by our ethics. Refusing to fall to the lesser things that the world attempts to lure us into or at times insists that we accept. All of this demands a fortitude and a prevailing conviction that consumes massive amounts of energy as well.

At some point, in some situation, in the face of some challenge we run squarely into the end of ourselves. We've attempted to avoid the inevitability of such a disheartening and frightening collision. And when it happens, we assume that there must be some resource, some bit of untapped energy, some reservoir yet undiscovered that we can draw from. But a time eventually comes where no such resource exists and we stand facing consuming circumstances with a depleted self.

In speaking to a bunch of exhausted people, Paul said that "God is able to bless you abundantly, so that in all things at all times, having all that you need, you will abound in every good work." This seemingly idealistic promise is what we're desperate to believe in. We want to know that the end of ourselves is never the end of our resources. That our weariness is obliterated by God's provision. That there is never a point nor a circumstance where our weariness can or will dictate our ability to overcome. And the amazing fact is, such a reality actually exists.

"Prayer is where my fatigue becomes
a stage upon which God can unveil His strength
in stunning fashion, and where my fear
is obliterated by His courage."
~ Craig D. Lounsbrough

Morning Prayer

Dear God:
I pretty much know what today will demand of me. It could be better or worse than I imagine as I sit here in the morning hours staring the coming day in the face. I don't know exactly what's out there, but something's out there and it will demand everything of me whether I have it to give or not.

I come to you with personal assets that won't be enough. They're just not enough. I'm living in a continual state of deficit. Dear God, it's really frightening to face the day knowing that what I must give is more than what I have to give. How to I produce what I don't have? How do I give what I don't have to give? And what am I supposed to do when these things are asked of me and I have to say no because there's nothing else I can say?

And so today I am claiming your promise that you will help me to "abound in every good work." Really abound. Not just get by. Not just deliver the bare minimum. Not dodge the proverbial bullet. No. I am asking for something immensely greater than that. Something wildly and incredibly supernatural. Something that is so not of myself that You are stunningly glorified. I am leaning into Your promise this morning. Your faithful and sure promise. And so today, I am looking for You to give me what I do not have.

I pray all of this in Jesus's Name. Amen

A Thought to Carry with Me Today

"It is not a matter of the size of the mountains that stand before us. For although the size of our faith might 'pale' in comparison, the size of our God handily 'impales' all comparisons."
~ *Craig D. Lounsbrough*

Before this day, I release to God...

_____

_____

_____

_____

_____

_____

Craig D. Lounsbrough

Evening Prayer

Dear God:
I made it. I'm here. With Your help I navigated the day. Thank you for providing me the resources necessary to meet the demands. Thank you for helping me understand that the end of myself is where You begin. And where You begin knows no ending. And the craziest thing of all is that You offer me the end of endings. Every day. In every circumstance. Regardless of the size of the challenges or how big the obstacles might be.

Tomorrow will come with its demands. That's what it does. And tonight I would ask that you would allow me to rest in the way that You would have me rest. I trust that You will grant me the exact rest that I need to face what's on the horizon of my tomorrow, knowing that You've already put the resources out in my tomorrow before that tomorrow ever becomes my today.

I pray all of this in Jesus' Name. Amen.

A Thought to Prepare for Tomorrow
"The things I'm burning daylight to figure out in my head are things God has already figured out in His. Faith then is resting in that fact, and in doing so suddenly finding out that among other things, I'm saving a whole bunch of daylight."
~ *Craig D. Lounsbrough*

90

From this day, I release to God...

_____

_____

_____

_____

_____

_____

_____

_____

_____

Day 6

I Can Do All Things Through Christ

"I can do all things through him
who gives me strength."
~ Philippians 4:13

We are bound by all kinds of limits. And we wonder why certain limits have to be limits. Why are our dreams stunted by limits that put them just outside of our reach? Why do we have relationships that become suffocated by limits, leaving them only a shadow of what they could be? Why do our job aspirations, our hopes for our children, our desires for a better world...why do all of these fall victim to limits that should not be limits?

We are a people of hope and vision. We can imagine great things. Incredible things. Fantastic stuff. We have the ability to visualize a greater good and a richer existence. We can craft fabulous dreams that are enriching beyond imagination. Yet, many of these fall prey to limitations that we did not create and cannot overcome. The best of ourselves and our dreams are often left languishing in the face of limits that thwart the best of us.

There seems to be a cruelty about it all. Something that borders on savagery. If our limits are going to cut the feet out from under our greatest dreams, why are we allowed to dream these things in the first place? Why a vision if limits render it impotent?

Limitations are not the issue. There's a vulnerability to every one of our limitations. A limit to our limitations. They are suspectable. They're not as ironclad and invincible as they would appear. And that's the reason that they exist. They exist to be broken. Not by us, but by the God Who breaks them daily. In the midst of the impossibilities that he faced,

Paul said, "I can do all things through him who gives me strength." That's the promise of limits broken and smashed. The promise of dreams safe to dream and visions worth having.

"I project my limits on God when faith would say that I should be projecting His limitlessness on me."
~ Craig D. Lounsbrough

Morning Prayer

Dear God:
I have to tell you that the limits look daunting. I'm surrounded by them. Every one of them looks insurmountable. I've run up against so many limits that have callously snuffed out so many of the things that I had hoped for and invested in. Limits have become the story of my life when I had hoped that my life would be a story of smashing limits.

God, I'm not afraid of limits. But I am afraid of what they do to me. They make it too risky to dream and hope and work. I'm afraid that I'll invest so much of myself into so many of the things that I'm so passionate about only to have them all coming to nothing. Limits kill. They crush. They disappoint. They give me a lot of apparently legitimate reasons not to hope. And those reasons become really convincing.

But I know that I need to rest in the fact that limits are never the end of any story. In fact, the greatest stories of all are those of limits defeated and dreams born. Those are the stories that You wish to tell in my life. The story of limits squashed, overcome, pressed off the pages of my life and obliterated. I can do all things through You. Help me to understand what "all things" means. And then help me to live it out with great faith and a stubbornly enduring hope.

I pray all of this in Jesus's Name. Amen

A Thought to Carry with Me Today
"If I'm not willing to accept a God who does the impossible, I'm left with what's possible. And that takes me no further than myself."
~ *Craig D. Lounsbrough*

Before this day, I release to God...

_____

_____

_____

_____

_____

_____

_____

_____

_____

Evening Prayer

Dear God:

I can look into tomorrow and I already know the limits that stand out there waiting for me to show up. I can also look inside of myself and see the limits within me that make the limits outside of me seem impenetrable. But wherever the limits are, they're all the same thing…limits.

I know that limits are more about what I believe them to be rather than what they actually are. I know that I give them strength and credibility because of the way that I think about them. I know that I empower them. I do that.

I can do all things through You. That makes the limits limited to what You want to do with them. Limits aren't barriers with You. They're faith builders, not dream crushers. They exist so that I can find myself elated when You've removed them. They give me the chance to watch You at work. To ruthlessly beat the limits into submission so that my dreams can rise to life itself. And because of all of that, I thank You for limits.

I pray all of this in Jesus' Name. Amen.

A Thought to Prepare for Tomorrow

"The idea is to always be attempting things that are greater than who I am. Otherwise I will never be more than who I am. That is why I prefer the call of God over

the plans of men, for the former is a call to the
impossible and the latter is a summons
To what I did yesterday."
~ Craig D. Lounsbrough

From this day, I release to God...

_____

_____

_____

_____

_____

_____

_____

_____

_____

Day 7

I Am Remarkably Made

*"I praise you because I am
fearfully and wonderfully made; your works
are wonderful, I know that full well."*
~ Psalm 139:14

That which we live with we take for granted by virtue of its familiarity to us. Its normality in our lives renders it unremarkable and bland. Anything precious, unique, or stunning is degraded by the familiarity that we have developed in our relationship with that thing.

The bane of familiarity and the manner in which it diminishes great things is most evident in our view of ourselves. We are the most common and regular things in our lives. We wake up with ourselves, spend the day with ourselves, and go to bed with ourselves. Such a subjective familiarity leaves us missing the wonder of our individuality and the beauty of our design.

We become the norm. Yes, we share many common traits with the rest of humanity. That renders us part of a larger story. But because of the predominance of those traits, the underlying uniqueness is swallowed up and rendered obscure. If we perceive any uniqueness we tend to attribute it to some global trait shared by all and thereby diminish it due to its commonality.

God says that you are "fearfully and wonderfully made." You are not the product of some sterile assembly-line process that rolls out identical products in some automated manner. God doesn't produce. He creates. You are the manifestation of God's genius and unlimited creativity. You are the embodiment of an artistry unmatched and a calling unique. You bear the imprint of God, and that can be nothing less than astounding.

*"Having spent the morning weeding, prunin
and bringing the garden to near perfection, I took a
moment to sit on the old garden bench to catch my
breath, brush the dirt from my hands, and wipe the
sweat from my brow. And scanning my handiwork, I
realized that I did not make the garden beautiful.
Rather, I just cleared away everything that had kept
the beauty from being seen. And I thought,
should we not do the same with our souls?"*

~ Craig D. Lounsbrough

Morning Prayer

Dear God:
The mirrors that I look into don't give me much back.
They're disappointing most of the time. The mirror of
my accomplishments is more about what hasn't
happened. The mirror of my past is either empty, or
disappointing, or both. The mirror of my dreams has
been wiped clean and left uninhabited. No matter how
I hold up these many mirrors, I'm not impressed with
myself at all.

But I know that mirrors do what I do…they reflect the
part of myself that matters the least. They call attention
to all that's truly unimportant. They draw conclusions
based on things that are not conclusive. They render me
void of the richness that they don't have the ability to
see. The immense beauty that You've implanted within
me. The gifting that lays ready to spring into action, and

the natural aptitudes that the world is in desperate need of. I am made to change the world, not just tolerate it. I have been vested with an array of unparalleled resources designed for the demands of our times. I am power waiting to be unleashed and beauty shared in the unleashing. Unleash me, dear God.

I pray all of this in Jesus's Name. Amen

A Thought to Carry with Me Today
"If you don't stop to take in the beauty around you, you will likewise miss the beauty within you."
~ *Craig D. Lounsbrough*

From this day, I release to God...

_____

_____

_____

_____

_____

_____

_____

_____

_____

_____

_____

Evening Prayer

Dear God:
I am a reflection of You. I carry Your image within me. That image resonates through every part of my being. No part of who I am is absent of Your character, Your nature, and Your essence. Dear God, please help me to understand that this can do nothing other than evidence how beautiful I am and how much I can do.

You know that I battle with a negative view of myself. You know that I have held the criticisms of others as true about who I am. You know that I have embodied those lies as part of my identity. And tonight I pray that You would purge those things out of me. Burn them out of me. Rip them out of me as lies about my true and eternal nature.

"I am fearfully and wonderfully made." As such, I give You praise. I thank You in a way that words can't express. Help me to embrace who You made me to be. Help me to rest in it, center myself upon it, and live it out with every breath that I take.

I pray all of this in Jesus' Name. Amen.

A Thought to Prepare for Tomorrow
"Maybe true beauty is when something quite 'simple' exercises whatever bit of faith it holds, and

in the exercising it suddenly discovers that the 'simple thing' that it always thought itself to be only served to hide the 'great thing' that it always was."

~ *Craig D. Lounsbrough*

From this day, I release to God...

_____

_____

_____

_____

_____

_____

_____

_____

Day 8

I Am Extraordinary

"So God created mankind in his own image,
in the image of God he created them; male
and female he created them."
~ Genesis 1:27

There's a normality that we assign to ourselves. We cultivate a sense of dreary commonality with other people. We draw off of what we see in others and utilize those insights to shape ourselves to the societal generalities around us. This allows us to more effectively mesh with the larger social dynamic that we circulate within. In essence, we become ordinary because being extraordinary is not an ordinary part of the society within which we wish to fit. Therefore, acceptance pillages individuality.

However, you are not the norm. Nor should you be. Life is not about blending in at the expense of our greater selves. To lose oneself in some societal concoction in order to gain acceptance is to pen a lifeless script for ourselves. In this blending we magnify the similarities that we have with others rather than cultivating the uniqueness that grants us the ability to help others claim their individuality. There is an immersion that categorizes our uniqueness as isolating rather than enriching. We find ourselves purging the extraordinary in favor of the mundaneness of social expectations and cultural mandates.

God did not create you to marginalize what He created. We are not designed to manage the uniqueness of ourselves into oblivion. The uniqueness that He built into you was not gifted to you as some socially isolating characteristic that you must rid yourself of. You are extraordinary. That uniqueness was not created as some 'best fit' for whatever might be societally vogue. Rather, it was crafted to intersect whatever the cultural climate might be in order to deliver a revolutionary transformation to that climate. And all of that is truly extraordinary.

"There are seeds of greatness within you.
You will either see them as worth planting, or you
will not. You may attempt to trade them for other seed
that will never adapt to the soil of your soul, or you
will realize that no seed created can match the ones
already within you. Wisdom would tell you to accept
the seeds, not your view of them. Prudence would
tell you to embrace the soil, not your sense of its
suitability. And determination would tell you to
rigorously cultivate that which is already within
you with great vigor, for to alter seed or soil
is to destroy both and render
the garden barren."
~ Craig D. Lounsbrough

Morning Prayer

Dear God:
I try to fit in. I suppose that most of us do that. I look at the world around me and I try to figure out my place in all of that. Where's my niche? If I can't find one, I try to create one. If I can't create one, I change myself to better fit one that already exists. I do a lot of this kind of thing.

And I know that I end up sacrificing my own uniqueness on the altar of lesser things. Whatever's extraordinary about me seems to be more isolating than anything else. It's something doesn't seem to fit in the places that I want to fit into. Or I don't believe that I possess anything extraordinary at all. And so I marginalize or deny those parts of myself. I ignore them, or rebuff them, or wish that I didn't have them. And I miss the fact that You gave me these things because these are the kinds of things that change the world. Help me to live that and understand that.

I pray all of this in Jesus's Name. Amen

A Thought to Carry with Me Today
"I was created for the simple reason that t not be created was unthinkable."
~ Craig D. Lounsbrough

From this day, I release to God...

_____

_____

_____

_____

_____

_____

_____

_____

_____

Dear God:
I'm trying to see that extraordinary part of myself. I know that it's there somewhere because You never created anyone who didn't have something extraordinary about them. I'm trying. And I'm working to accept the fact that some of those things might put me outside of the places that I would like to be in. They might set me on the periphery of the social circles that I long to be a part of or exclude me from them altogether.

But I know that those extraordinary things weren't made to fit those circles. That's the point. They were meant to transform them. That's why I have them. I know that things that force-fit themselves into some dynamic never change the things that they're force-fitting themselves into. They must become those things and that renders them impotent. I don't want to become 'things.' I want to change things. I mean really change things. And the unique gifting that You have given me, and the things about me that are truly extraordinary are the very things that change things. Never, never allow me to sacrifice the wonder of who and what You made me to be.

I pray all of this in Jesus' Name. Amen.

A Thought to Prepare for Tomorrow

"The horse-drawn plow sat engulfed in weeds at the
edge of the field. And while it had stopped plowing
long ago, it never left the place where it had plowed.
And I thought that if we leave what we were
created to do, we are likely to forget who
we were created to be."
~ Craig D. Lounsbrough

From this day, I release to God...

_____

_____

_____

_____

_____

_____

_____

_____

Day 9

I Am Provided For

"His divine power has given us everything we need for a godly life through our knowledge of him who called us by his own glory and goodness."
~ *2 Peter 1:3*

We walk with a gnawing sense of deficits. Those might be material things. They could be relationships. It's possible that they're our self-esteem, or a lack of courage, an absence of vision, or an inability to fight the depression in our lives. We might feel inadequate to face the challenges, overcome the obstacles, beat our debt, crush our addictions, or simply live a meaningful life. We walk with a gnawing sense of deficits.

Or we've discovered that life itself is inadequate. It doesn't possess what it promises. It's the great snake-oil salesman offering miracle cures with sugar-water marketing schemes. Therefore we adjust our expectations, marginalize our lives, forfeit our passions, gut our dreams, and eek out some pathetic existence because neither we nor the world is adequate to any of them. We become defined by what we don't have rather than by what we do.

Let's be clear. God is not a God of deficits. Deficits are the absence of God and the presence of sin. Despite the size of them, deficits are never the end of anything. In fact, if God has allowed us to walk bound by deficits, it's simply because the growth that will arise out of wrestling with those deficits will crush those deficits and release everything that those deficits led us to believe was impossible.

In the midst of his own deficits as well as the inadequacies of his world, Paul boldly said, "My God will meet all of your needs according to the riches of his glory in Christ Jesus." There's no room for any deficit in that promise. Yes, we walk with a gnawing sense of deficits. But we walk with a God Who promises that every deficit that we carry is living its own death sentence.

"I will most certainly focus on one of two things; the nagging deficits of my handicap, or the masterful honing brought about by my handicap. And my choice of focus will determine if my handicap will remain a handicap."
~ Craig D. Lounsbrough

Morning Prayer

Dear God:
All that I tend to see is what I'm not and what the world is not. I let these deficits define me. I let them dictate how I view myself and my life. I know that I've let them become my story. It's hard not to let them dominate everything that I think about. I've given them way too much power.

I know that I let these deficits kill my hopes and stifle my dreams. They suck the air out of my life every day, with every dream lost and every hope shattered. And far too often I stand here feeling defeated by all of the stuff that I feel is telling me that it's not worth it. Why try? Or, it's better to give up now rather than work your fingers to the bone trying to do something that will fail after you've invested the whole of yourself into it. My deficits and those in the world around me are killing me because I've let them do that.

God, there is no deficit in You. Not one. You are complete and total in every way. Every way! And You offer that wholeness to me. You offer me a life so complete, so comprehensive, so vibrantly total in every way that no deficit has the ability to stay a deficit.

And so, today I am asking You to remind me that there is no deficit in You. None. And that You stand ready to bring that kind of deficit-free fullness into my life. Remind me that every deficit is an opportunity for growth that will eventually smash every deficit. Remind me today and every day that You are the God of deficit-less fullness.

I pray all of this in Jesus's Name. Amen

A Thought to Carry with Me Today
"Deficits are defeated by the strength that I gain in fighting them."
~ *Craig D. Lounsbrough*

Before this day, I release to God...

_____

_____

_____

_____

_____

_____

Evening Prayer

Dear God:

For every deficit that I have, I possess many more strengths that have more than ample ability to wipe out those deficits. I know that this is true. And those strengths are from You. You gifted me with those. But what's even more amazing is that You've gifted me with strengths that I haven't even recognized yet. Within me You've put strengths and abilities that are just waiting to emerge and press the deficits in my life and my world right out of my life and my world. I know that You created me to be bigger than everything that would work to destroy me. That's genius! Absolute genius! Thank you for making me that way.

Tonight, I go to bed asking You to strengthen those strengths beyond what I can even imagine. And then I'm asking You to take the strengths that I haven't yet discovered and begin the incredible process of laying them out in front of me. Dear God, there is no deficit in You. Mold me and shape me to be as deficit-less as You are.

I pray all of this in Jesus' Name. Amen.

A Thought to Prepare for Tomorrow
"Deficits only survive if we grant them permission to be the lie that allows them to be deficits."
~ Craig D. Lounsbrough

From this day, I release to God...

_____

_____

_____

_____

_____

_____

_____

_____

_____

Day 10

I Am Valuable

"For you know that it was not with perishable things such as silver or gold that you were redeemed from the empty way of life handed down to you from your ancestors, but with the precious blood of Christ, a lamb without blemish or defect."
~ 1 Peter 1:18-19

The world is not predisposed to affirm us. We are more the stuff of a commodity to be bartered. Our value is tied to our productivity. And if that productivity doesn't parallel the things that the world has determined to have value, neither does that productivity. As with any commodity, if we are not viewed as contributing to the societal good as determined by whatever dictates might be trending at that moment, we are discarded.

This dynamic plays itself out in families, businesses, communities, relationships, and in any place where people dictate the nature and form of the entity. If in some manner we do not adhere to whatever the established dictates might be, we have no value to that organization or system. Therefore, we are discarded in favor of those who are willing to walk in lockstep with those systems and their criteria. And since those people will always exist, being discarded is never more than a step away.

Conversely, our value to God is not based on our adherence. Our value is based on the fact that we are created in His image. We have that bit of God within us. That forever DNA. We possess that infinite genetic component whose essence is eternal. We can move in unison with this God whose identity we share, or we can reject Him entirely. Either way, we are held with an infinite love. Jesus said, "...even the very hairs of your head are all numbered." His love for us is so understanding that no detail of our lives (despite how small they might be) are missed. God's love is tedious, persistent, far-reaching, all-enveloping, and entirely attentive. Everything about us matters whether or not God matters to us. That's love.

"God is precise, deliberate and intentional. Therefore, everything He created held sufficient value for Him to create it. And of all things, that includes you."
~ Craig D. Lounsbrough

Morning Prayer

Dear God:
I try to fit in. But I've figured out that fitting in always compromises who I am. There's some part of me I have to hide, or discard, or deny in order to fit in. I lose parts of me I shouldn't have to lose. The cost to me is always greater than any acceptance that I might gain. And even if I am accepted, that's going to shift based on whatever's vogue or trending. As soon as what I've become is no longer a fit, I'm discarded again.

Dear God, I sometimes wonder if I have any value in just being me. Just me. Nothing else or nobody else. It doesn't seem that way most of the time. I feel like a commodity that's bartered based on my perceived value. I live in the fear of wondering when I'm going to be deemed as outmoded and of no use. When will I be discarded next?

But You embrace me always. You might find my behaviors damaging. You might be grieved by the things that I chase after. Your heart may have been broken by me more times than my heart could take if You were the one doing the breaking. But whether I embrace You or reject You, I remain of incalculable to You. And even though I can't always explain it, I am grateful that I am that valuable to You.

I pray all of this in Jesus's Name. Amen

A Thought to Carry with Me Today

"How do I begin to evaluate my worth? By realizing that some things can't be assigned a value, and that my life is one of them."
~ *Craig D. Lounsbrough*

Before this day, I release to God...

_____

_____

_____

_____

_____

_____

Evening Prayer

Dear God:
The world kind of beat me up today. It walked on me. At times, it walked past me as if I were invisible to it. It frowned upon me because I wasn't exactly what it

wanted me to be. And when the world does that, I can't help but walk away with some sense that I don't matter. That I have no value. That I'm of no consequence to anything or anybody.

But tonight I'm asking that You remind me of my worth. Help me to look past the actions and the choices of a world that doesn't even value itself. Help me to root my sense of worth and value in You. To really root that in You because You and You alone define my worth and value. The world can't do that, even though it arrogantly claims the ability to do so. And You say that my worth is evidenced by the death of Your Son. That is a worth that I desperately wish to embrace with the whole of myself. Help me to do so.

I pray all of this in Jesus' Name. Amen.

A Thought to Prepare for Tomorrow
"I am a one-of-a-kind manifestation of God's creative genius so pristinely unique that it will never be repeated in all of time and history. And while the world might devalue me in ways rogue and brutal, and while I too frequently do the same, my worth simply cannot be touched."
~ Craig D. Lounsbrough

Taking It to Our Knees

From this day, I release to God...

_____

_____

_____

_____

_____

_____

_____

_____

Day 11

I Am Chosen

"You did not choose me, but I chose you and appointed you so that you might go and bear fruit— fruit that will last—and so that whatever you ask in my name the Father will give you."
~ John 15:16

We desperately want to be chosen. Desperately. We want someone to press all of the other options aside, point directly at us and say, "I choose you." We were their choice. In the middle of all of the other people, or all of the selections that were available to them, they singled us out and picked us. They narrowed down all of the options, weighed them carefully and said, "I want you." We want to be chosen.

Being chosen communicates to us that we have enough value to be held above all of the other options. We possessed something worthy enough to be set apart. To be elevated. To be singled out. We have a value that distinguishes us as unique, gifted, markedly equipped, and possessing an intelligence that equips us to utilize these resources effectively and efficiently. Being chosen is potently affirming.

But many times we are not chosen. Sometimes we don't even get the slightest nod or barest acknowledgement. Sometimes we're passed over with not so much as a glance in our direction. Many times we're not chosen. Many times we're not even considered.

God says, "I choose you." The immensity of that choice rests in what He's chosen you to do. The fruit that He's designed you to bear. He's chosen you to change your world. Not just passively reside in it or touch it here and there when it's convenient. No. He's chosen you for great things. Phenomenal things. Things that have eternal implications that you can't even see from where you're standing. That's what you've been chosen for. And what a privilege to be chosen for something as massive as that!

> *"Maybe we were chosen because it*
> *Grants us the power to choose another who*
> *needs to be chosen worse than we do."*
> *~ Craig D. Lounsbrough*

Morning Prayer

Dear God:
Thank You for choosing me. Thank You. Yes, I want to be chosen. I need to be chosen. I need to know that I possess something worth choosing. But maybe more than that, being chosen means that I have a job. A calling. A purpose. Being chosen means that I was chosen 'for' something. My life has meaning. It just doesn't end with me because that's a pretty small ending. Being chosen by You means that there's mission bigger than me. A mission to change things. To transform things. To make things better.

Lord, I've been passed over many times. Many, many times. At other times I was chosen, but then I was abandoned. I was unchosen. I was considered worthy, but then that assessment was reversed and withdrawn. And I live with those wounds yet today.

But You chose me because You created me to be chosen. You endowed me with a richness that You will never overlook because You can't. You chose me not for one day, or two, or a month, or a year. You chose me for eternity. Your choice of me will never be undone or reversed. And so, thank You for choosing me, but not only choosing me. Thank You for choosing me to do incredible things in a world that is in need of incredible things.

I pray all of this in Jesus's Name. Amen

A Thought to Carry With Me Today

"Dear God, choose me for something
that the world (with all of its resources) hasn't been
able to accomplish. For such a task as this would fill
me with a fear of the task but ignite me with a
passion that would crush the fear
sufficiently to crush the task."
~ *Craig D. Lounsbrough*

Before this day, I release to God...

_____

_____

_____

_____

_____

_____

_____

_____

_____

Evening Prayer

Dear God:
I choose You. I know that You have chosen me. And even though I don't understand that sometimes, even though I can't comprehend it, I'm grateful that You did. But tonight, I declare yet again that I choose You. This night and every night.

And in choosing You, I surrender myself to Your choices for me. What do You want me to do? What role to You want me to play in all of this? Where's my spot. What's my mission? What am I supposed to give my life over to? Dear God, tell me what that is and I will do it. I might fear it. I might find my cowardice building some great hesitation within me. I have no doubt that I'm going to see it as bigger than who I am and greater than any resources that I might have to get it done. But right now, tonight, I choose to accept You and whatever You call me to do. I am Yours. Tonight and every night.

I pray all of this in Jesus' Name. Amen.

A Thought to Prepare for Tomorrow
"If you have a hard time believing that God chose you, it's probably because you haven't chosen you."
~ Craig D. Lounsbrough

Taking It to Our Knees

From this day, I release to God...

_____

_____

_____

_____

_____

_____

_____

_____

Craig D. Lounsbrough

Day 12

I Am Courageous

*"Be strong and courageous. Do not be afraid or terrified because of them, for the L

ORD your God goes with you; he will never leave you nor forsake you."*
~ *Deuteronomy 31:6*

Courage might be something that we desire, but it's something that we don't have much of. We can imagine ourselves as courageous. We can play out a thousand different scenarios where we take a bold stance against a great adversary. We imagine ourselves saving the day, rushing to the rescue, turning the tide, and saving the world. Yet when imagination gives way to reality, we cower, turn tail, and we run.

Courage is less a state of mind or character. Rather, it's a decision. It's a choice to intentionally place oneself at great risk on behalf of someone else. It's a decision against self-preservation. It's an action whereby we press ourselves aside in favor of something greater than ourselves. Courage in action is sacrifice on display. It's the essence of our humanity acting on that essence.

Yet, cowardice is pesky. It seems that it has a death grip on our humanity. It preaches retreat. It enlists fear as a proponent against sacrifice. It declares self-preservation as the fullest expression of our humanity.

Yes, cowardice is pesky.

Yet, God calls us to intimately courageous living. And He does so by declaring that we are never courageous alone. We never stand alone. The Bible says, "the LORD your God goes with you." With you. Alongside of you. In front of you and behind you. Saving the day, rushing to the rescue, turning the tide, and saving the world are never solitary endeavors. We do these things with the Infinite God standing at our side. And when we act on that reality, cowardice is wiped clean by the courage we've always hoped to have.

"Strip away all self-interest, embrace self-sacrifice as the noblest of all pursuits, see your existence as the asset that amplifies the existence of another; embrace these things and courage will finally have a place to be courageous."
~ Craig D. Lounsbrough

Morning Prayer

Dear God:
I guess I'm courageous enough to admit that I'm not courageous. I suppose that's a start. But I want more. I don't want to live a life where I'm out there doing crazy stuff or being reckless. I don't want that. But I want to possess a courage that allows me to step into situations that are difficult, risky, or even dangerous.

And I know that any thin shred of courage that I might have doesn't rest in me, for that's the fantasy that I've created to offset the disappointing reality that I'm more a coward than anything else. If I am courageous at all, it's because You stand beside me. It's because You boldly go before me and You stand immovable behind me. It's because You hem me in, and You lay Your hand upon me. That's what makes me brave. It's Your committed companionship that gives me what I don't have.

And so today, I go into the world out there emboldened with the courage that comes from knowing that I'm not going out there alone. You are everywhere around me. You are already in places I haven't even gotten to yet. And You are in the places I've already been. You are everywhere with me. And today I embrace and live those realities.

I pray all of this in Jesus's Name. Amen

A Thought to Carry with Me Today
"The height of the tree is never measured in feet.
Rather, it is measured by the courage of those who
seek to climb it. Therefore, one tree can
have many heights."
~ Craig D. Lounsbrough

Before this day, I release to God…

_____

_____

_____

_____

_____

_____

_____

Evening Prayer

Dear God:

My courage came and went today. There were times when I felt courageous. And then there were times when I didn't feel that at all. I'm fickle when it comes to courage. I know that some things are riskier than others. Some things are more daunting, or more pressing, or more dangerous. And the level of my courage seems to be a barometer that's based on the gravity of whatever it is that I'm facing.

Dear God, I want my courage to be courageous regardless of what I face. I stand with You because You stand with me. And that invincible bond remains untouched regardless of what it is that I'm facing. And so, help me to stand on the fact that You stand with me. And whatever it is that I'm standing against has no hope of standing against us. Help me to know that to the very core of my being.

I pray all of this in Jesus' Name. Amen.

A Thought to Prepare for Tomorrow
"The greatest act of strength is to acknowledge that we have none. The greatest act of faith is to believe that our weakness is God's strength. And the greatest act of courage is to act on these realities."
~ Craig D. Lounsbrough

From this day, I release to God…

_____

_____

_____

_____

_____

_____

_____

_____

Day 13

I Am a Conqueror

"No, in all these things we are more than conquerors through him who loved us."
~ Romans 8:37

Defeat is never far away, nor is the fear of it. We tend to look at the challenges in our lives less based on the probability of success, and more on the likelihood of defeat. We're negatively predisposed. Defeat is a sore spot for most of us. We've had plenty of it. We live with a deep aversion to stepping into anything that has even the slightest scent of defeat about it. The tiniest hint of it (or possibility of it) and we're out.

For us, defeat is a direct and rather biting commentary on our worth, our value, our ability, and our intelligence. Defeat is not just about the defeat itself, whatever that might have been. It's about the corrosive mindset that follows hot on its heels. The best of ourselves fell short. Our energies were insufficient. Our creativity too dull. Our ingenuity was anything but. And being risk-averse, we press great things aside and invest in the mundaneness of that which presents no real challenge.

We have dreams. However, most of our dreams die before they had a chance to be born. And that happens because we don't see ourselves as conquerors. On a good day we might call ourselves explorers, feeling out the possibilities of some vision. But to step onto the path with a commitment to the journey requires the belief that we can conquer the dream rather than having defeat conquer us.

Paul said that we are "more than conquerors." We are "more" than people who can simply overcome or achieve. We are "more" than that. Conquering is not the issue. The issue is 'what' we will conquer. Not 'if' we will conquer. The issue is figuring out what God is calling us to conquer and doing the conquering in a manner that's utterly decisive and life-altering. It's to conquer the unconquerable as an indisputable testimony to what God can do through a person who's sold out to Him.

"Once our fears are conquered, what was once a mighty storm becomes a passing drizzle."
~ Craig D. Lounsbrough

Morning Prayer

Dear God:
My dream is to conquer. I want to conquer the lesser things about me. I want to conquer the attitudes and behaviors that claim to have conquered me. I want to conquer the pain in my history. The trauma that haunts me. The damaged self-esteem that's always touting my inabilities and holding them up in front of my face. I want to conquer my fear of relationships, the depression that darkens my day, and the anxiety that shuts me down every day. I want to conquer all of this. I want to crush it.

But dear God, my dream is bigger than that. I want to conquer the things in my world that You're calling me to conquer. I mean, there's some huge things out there that I know You're calling me to. Some really massive stuff. Your purpose for me is to conquer. To overcome. To vanquish. To eliminate.

But You said that I am 'more' than a conqueror. That means that I just don't beat things or destroy them. I take them one step further. I transform them. I change them. I turn them from enemies to friends. From that which is toxic to that which is life-giving. I turn that which is destructive to something gloriously constructive. And that is what I will do today.

I pray all of this in Jesus's Name. Amen

A Thought to Carry with Me Today
"History will not praise those that
conquered nations through use of force. Rather,
history will praise those who conquered hearts, for
that is how you conquer nations."
~ Craig D. Lounsbrough

Before this day, I release to God...

_____

_____

_____

_____

_____

_____

_____

Evening Prayer

Dear God:
I conquered some things today. Some of that didn't go all that well, and some went really well. Then there were things that conquered me, or at least got the best of me.

I want tomorrow to be a day of conquering. Give me that mindset. But more than just the mindset of being a conqueror, give me a mindset of faith so that the mindset of conquering is radically emboldened by my faith in You as the ultimate conqueror. Help me to see what You want me to conquer today. And then, help me to see the manner in which You want it conquered, for conquering is not about vanquishing or destroying something. It's about changing it radically. It's about making it what it never was so that it can do a great good that it never could have done. Empower me to conquer like that. Like You did in sending Your Son. Like You do yet today. Help me to conquer in order to save, for that is the best kind of conquering imaginable.

I pray all of this in Jesus' Name. Amen.

A Thought to Prepare for Tomorrow
"The victory was sealed at an empty tomb. Therefore, we must remember that the remaining battles are victory concluding, not victory in question."
~ Craig D. Lounsbrough

From this day, I release to God...

_____

_____

_____

_____

_____

_____

_____

_____

Day 14

I Am Strong

"Even youths grow tired and weary, and young men stumble and fall; but those who hope in the LORD will renew their strength. They will soar on wings like eagles; they will run and not grow weary, they will walk and not be faint."
~ Isaiah 40:30-31

Strength is a lot of things. But there are a lot of things that it is not. We have a rather rogue tendency to confuse strength with lesser things like stubbornness, ignorance, selfishness, advocating for misdirected philosophies, standing for misguided morality, or heeding the persuasive voice of greed. We tend to label these things as strength.

In fact, strength is exercising the choice not to exercise these things. True strength is to vigorously stand against the things that the world declares as strengths. Much more than that however, it is our determination not to 'be' those things. True strength, authentic strength is the ability to look within and to ruthlessly purge out all of the things within us that cause us to act like the world around us.

To do the right things, the deep things, the hard things, the transforming things will demand strength. They will demand a strength born of courage, weaned on sacrifice, energized by vision, and resting firm on faith. True strength is the deliberate accumulation of things bigger than us and the insertion of those things within us.

And all of that rests in a God Who wants us to run with great speed and soar to greater heights. A strength that creates an unstoppable momentum. A strength that renders passivity bleak and sour. A strength that exposes the world's strength as the fraud that it is. We are crafted to receive just such a strength. And we are designed to unleash that strength into everything that is begging for someone of strength to step in and transform them in and through that strength. Through God, that exact strength is ours!

"The greatest act of strength is to acknowledge that we have none. The greatest act of faith is to believe that our weakness is God's strength. And the greatest act of courage is to act on these realities."
~ Craig D. Lounsbrough

Morning Prayer

Dear God:
I am not strong. At times I tell myself that I am. And sometimes I even act like I'm strong. But my sense of strength is more the desire for strength than the actual possession of it.

But I don't want to be strong just to be strong because then any strength that I have becomes self-serving. And that kind of strength is never really strength. I don't want that. What I want is a strength that changes the things within me that need to be changed simply because that's the first and only step to changing the things around me. Give me the strength for a world that needs me to be strong. Give me strength for friends whose lives are collapsing, neighbors whose lives have collapsed, for the needs represented in my community, and the pain pressing itself through my family. Give me the strength to bring Your healing to all of these so that Your Kingdom might be advanced in each of them.

I pray all of this in Jesus's Name. Amen

A Thought to Carry with Me Today
"Strength is what is granted to me by God
so that He might show through me what He
Wishes to do through others."
~ *Craig D. Lounsbrough*

Before this day, I release to God…

_____

_____

_____

_____

Evening Prayer

Dear God:
Whatever strength I had this morning was spent on
what I did today. It's amazing what the world demands
of me the minute that I step out of that door. The world
immediately descends upon me demanding whatever it
might choose to demand. It always wants something.
Always. And it seems to me that by the time I give it
what it's demanding of me, I have nothing left to
demand something of it.

Dear God, I want a strength that is never fatigued by
the world. In fact, I want a strength that never ceases to

143

exceed what the world demands of me. But more than that, I want a strength that can say "no" to the demands that should have never been made of me or of others. I want to change the world and not be changed by it. So, give me a renewed strength tonight so that I can do something to change the world tomorrow. Renew me physically tonight. Renew me mentally, emotionally, and spiritually. And in that renewal, I want to get up tomorrow with a strength from You that I can't even imagine in order to change a world that needs to be changed in ways that I can't imagine.

I pray all of this in Jesus' Name. Amen.

A Thought to Prepare for Tomorrow
"It wasn't the sunrise that took my breath away. Rather, it was the privilege of knowing that forces a billion times my own strength silently merged in the first light of a new day to remind me that I am part of something infinitely bigger than all of the combined challenges of any day."
~ Craig D. Lounsbrough

From this day, I release to God...

_____

_____

_____

_____

Day 15

I Am Forgiven

*"If we confess our sins, he is faithful
And just and will forgive us our sins and
purify us from all unrighteousness."*
~ 1 John 1:9

God says that we are forgiven. He says that very plainly and His actions evidence that statement quite pointedly. You can't miss it. But, we don't feel it. Not really.

The nature of our decisions were such that they simply can't be put to rest. The gravity of whatever we've done often requires some sort of corrective action that is larger than the offense that such an action seeks to free us of. And that means that we ourselves are unable to generate an action capable of pulling that off. We become stuck in the consequences of whatever it was that we shouldn't have done.

Essentially this means acknowledging that the consequences of our actions exceed our ability to rectify those consequences. We don't have the ability nor the resources to bring something superior to the outcomes generated by our choices. It's one thing to offer some sort of penance, as genuine as that might be. But it's quite another thing to create something restorative that exceeds the offense itself. That's beyond us.

Therefore, there must be something bigger than us that can rectify what we cannot. God forgives, but He moves far beyond that. He "purifies us from all unrighteousness." God does a work that far exceeds the offense. A purification that transforms. God does not simply release us from what we've done. He transforms who we are. And that transformation not only puts us in perfect stead with God, but it also positions us away from the things that drove us to the original actions. This is what God offers our every offense.

"Forgiveness is telling ourselves that the 'wrong' that we did will not impede the 'right' that we can do."
~ Craig D. Lounsbrough

Morning Prayer

Dear God:
I sit in my own guilt. It's not that I want to. It's that I can't shake it. However, I guess that sometimes I might sit in it because I feel that I deserve to be punished, in whatever way I think that I'm doing that. But I sit in my guilt.

I know that You don't want me to be here. If You did, You wouldn't have created a way for me to get out of it. I'm not stuck here because of You. I'm stuck here because of me. I've sentenced myself to this somehow thinking that it will make things right in my head. But it doesn't. It never will.

I confess the things that I've done. I did them, and I shouldn't have. I was short-sighted. I was greedy. I was afraid. What I was doesn't justify what I did. And so I'm asking for Your forgiveness. But I'm also asking that I feel it. I want to know it. To be certain of it. And as You do that, I want You to purify me. Make me the person who will never make those choices again because they are no longer who I am. Put me so far beyond that place that I will never grieve another choice in that way, and I will never bear this kind of guilt ever again. And finally, or maybe first, heal the people that I hurt. May what they see in me help them heal from the wounds that I inflicted on them.

I pray all of this in Jesus's Name. Amen

A Thought to Carry with Me Today
"Forgiveness brilliantly rewrites the script that we've penned to process the pain and betrayal of our histories. And while such a rewrite does not change history itself, it changes everything about our history."
~ Craig D. Lounsbrough

Before this day, I release to God...

_____

_____

_____

_____

Evening Prayer

Dear God:
This evening I seek forgiveness for the foolish choices that I made today. I did some dumb stuff. But help me to understand that I made some good choices too. Some really good choices, in fact.

But I don't want to keep score because You don't. That just compares me with myself and that doesn't go very far. Instead I want to focus on joining You in the purification that You are working out in my life. Your purification is perfect, but I am not. And I know that I am slow to learn at times, and resistant at others. But I thank You that Your forgiveness of me isn't deterred by either. Your forgiveness exceeds my ability to receive it or work it out in my life. Your forgiveness is not bound by my weakness or lackluster determination. Your forgiveness is as complete as You are. And tonight I embrace those truths with the commitment to live them out in every tomorrow.

I pray all of this in Jesus' Name. Amen.

A Thought to Prepare for Tomorrow
"Forgiveness is an action where our lesser selves
decide to be more than less."
~ Craig D. Lounsbrough

From this day, I release to God...

_____

_____

_____

_____

_____

_____

Craig D. Lounsbrough

Day 16

I Am Blameless

*"Therefore, if anyone is in Christ,
the new creation has come. The old
has gone, the new is here!"*
~ 2 Corinthians 5:17

150

Our identity is often centered on sorting out the mess of who we are. And that sorting is often based on the belief that the first step in being 'new' is cleaning up the 'old.' We've got to tidy things up first. We've got to beat the addiction. Heal from the divorce. Grieve the job loss. Make amends with our kids. We've got to sort this stuff out.

God doesn't clean up messes. He ends them. God isn't walking around picking up the pieces in the places where we used to be. Paul says, "The old is gone." Gone. That stuff's not there. Neither is the place where all of it used to be piled up. It's gone.

Paul says that "the new creation has come." God is the embodiment of all beginnings. He is the origin of all things. God's beginnings are not a continuation of anything. We shed everything that kept us old. The sin, the choices, the behaviors, the attitudes, the failures, the insecurities...all of the stuff that wrecked us. We can leave the past in a place where it will never be repeated because we have become the people who won't repeat what we no longer are.

"The new creation has come." In force. With an eternal intentionality. With a vigor empowered by God and enamored by the vision of ourselves that He has given us. And if we are to be blamed for anything it would be for a faith that would dare us to believe that we can shed the addiction, the divorce, the job loss, and the damage that we did to our kids. "The new is here," and blame vanished at the very moment that the 'new' showed up.

"A 'new start' is where I tediously reconstruct everything I've spent most of my life destroying. A 'fresh start' is where God hands me something I've haven't had the chance to destroy. And while I am free to choose either one, the former is a life repurposed while the latter is a life reborn."
~ Craig D. Lounsbrough

Morning Prayer

Dear God:
I'm not asking that You make me blameless. I'm asking that You make me new. And I'm asking you to make me new in such a way that I will no longer be blamed for what no longer exists within me. The old self is gone. Not buried. Not incarcerated within the walls of its many mistakes. Not waiting for some moment to burst back on the stage of my life. Rather, help me to understand that its existence has been wiped out.

Break me of the habit of holding onto a past that is no longer there to hold onto. Purge me of the inclination to believe that what existed within me has preserved some small part of itself and that it's sitting off in some dark corner slowly piecing itself back together again. Help me understand that there are no pieces and no corners.

And finally, if I'm ever blamed for anything, might I be blamed for not sufficiently cultivating the 'new' that You are bringing about in me. Might any blame be that I have impeded such a grand work. And in light of any such blame, might I recommit to everything that You are working out in my life.

I pray all of this in Jesus's Name. Amen

A Thought to Carry with Me Today

"God has no interest in doing some slick revisions or innovative tweaks in order to make transformation feel measured and safe. Rather, He's about delivering a sweeping overhaul to your life that will leave nothing untouched and everything transformed. Therefore, the question regarding transformation is whether we're brave enough to experience the transformation from which we cannot return but cannot miss."
~ Craig D. Lounsbrough

Before this day, I release to God...

_____

_____

_____

_____

_____

_____

Evening Prayer

Dear God:
I am a new person in an old world. There's some conflict in that for me. I wonder how I make my 'new' fit into everything that's 'old.' That's tough. But help to understand that it's not about fitting my 'new' into an 'old' world. Instead it's about engaging an 'old' world in order to make that world 'new.' And that world includes me.

I know that what I've become is what the world needs. But dear God, help me to be the 'new' that the world is out there aimlessly looking for. Put me in places where the world see's the 'new.' I don't know that I'm the kind of person who wants to flaunt who You've made me to be. And I don't think that the people in the world would find that very appealing anyway. Just help me to live out this 'new' in a manner that's entirely natural, completely comfortable, irresistibly appealing, and free of the blame that the 'new' has eradicated.

I pray all of this in Jesus' Name. Amen.

A Thought to Prepare for Tomorrow
"Transformation that is neither fiercely turbulent nor inordinately frightening is not transformation."
~ Craig D. Lounsbrough

From this day, I release to God...

_____

_____

_____

_____

_____

_____

_____

_____

Day 17

I Am Fearless

"For the Spirit God gave us does not make us timid, but gives us power, love and self-discipline."
~ 2 Timothy 1:7

The notion is that being fearless has something tirelessly heroic about. It brings to mind courageous people standing in the fray of monumental moments filled with horror and impending risk. We know that the tables of history itself tipped on those precarious moments when men and women of great courage and fearlessness cast safety to the wind and marched into the battles. There's something bold and brazen in their actions that we would like to see manifest in our own lives. Such actions would thrust our humanity to great heights and thereby anoint our existence.

But these are the few. We might believe in our ability to understand their fearlessness. However, the potent rawness of their bravery is entirely unknown to us until we are thrust into horrific situations where the nature of our character is laid bare. And in those heated moments we discover that the fearlessness that we covet often eludes us and we stand embarrassed in our cowardice.

But being fearless does not rise or fall on who we are, but on Who we stand with. Being fearless is choosing to be a conduit through which God funnels His "power, love and self-discipline." Endowed with the raw potency of these qualities we find ourselves infused with a fearlessness that shrinks the adversary and fires our courage. God made us to be fearless. That's part of our coding. Infused with His power and ignited by His passions, being fearless is woven into our very nature. And that completely shifts our view of ourselves as held against the challenges in our world.

Craig D. Lounsbrough

*"Many adventurers would say that
opportunity is something that you find as part
of a relentless search, or that it's something that an
imagination unleashed shapes and creates. And while
all of that sounds bold and wonderfully fearless, it's
my sense that opportunity is more that thing to which
we've been called by something larger than ourselves,
and less something that is a product of ourselves."
~ Craig D. Lounsbrough*

Morning Prayer

Dear God:
I live most of my life cowering from life. Yeah, I'm out there doing what I have to do. And at times that might look fearless to people who can't see the fear that's running rampant across the tundra of my soul. Yet most times I am anything but fearless.

Today I claim the fact that a life of fear is not the story that You have penned for me. You have made provision for me to live fearlessly. You have crafted my entire being in a manner that the infusion of "power, love and self-discipline" thrusts me above that which would seek to intimidate me and crush me.

Therefore, I am praying the force of "power, love and self-discipline" into my life. I don't know what I might face today. However, whatever that might be, press the force of "power, love and self-discipline" into to the core of my being that I might rise up in the face of great adversity and be the person I long to be and am destined to be.

I pray all of this in Jesus's Name. Amen

A Thought to Carry with Me Today
"Strip away all self-interest, embrace self-sacrifice
as the noblest of all pursuits, see your existence as the
asset that amplifies the existence of another; embrace
these things and courage will finally have a
place to be courageous."
~ Craig D. Lounsbrough

Before this day, I release to God...

_____

_____

_____

_____

_____

_____

Evening Prayer

Dear God:
Tomorrow is another opportunity to be fearless. I'm not necessarily looking for opportunities, but if You should choose to bring them my way, help me to stand faithfully in the face of them. But if I truly wish to be

fearless, then maybe I need to ask You to bring those opportunities. To pray that You bring them. That You bring them to make me fearless by standing in the face of the things that strike me with fear.

And so, my prayer tonight is three-fold. Bring the challenges my way. Bring them. In whatever way You bring them or in whatever manner You permit them to come...bring them. Secondly, infuse me with Your "power, love and self-discipline" as I stand facing them. And thirdly, as You have promised, I ask You to stand before me, behind me, and around me in a manner that my courage rests not in me, but in the God in Who surrounds me with His relentless invincibility.

I pray all of this in Jesus' Name. Amen.

A Thought to Prepare for Tomorrow
"God will never allow a flood in Your life without providing you a boat within which the storm itself feels absent and the waves calm."
~ Craig D. Lounsbrough

From this day, I release to God...

_____

_____

_____

_____

_____

Day 18

I Am Blessed

"Praise be to the God and Father of our Lord Jesus Christ, who has blessed us in the heavenly realms with every spiritual blessing in Christ."
~ Ephesians 1:3

We have a rather flimsy definition of what it is to be blessed. It appears that this lackluster definition of ours is based on the widely accepted cultural definitions of what a blessing is. Those definitions are colored dim by the shallowness of the culture that created them. In reality, we have humanized the idea and therefore we hold it hostage to a pathetically weakened ideal.

Therefore, we are driven to achieve things in our careers, or our marriages, or our friendships, or our lives as means of obtaining these shallow and pithy blessings. Given the inherently shallow nature of these blessings, they are neither sustainable nor firm. Therefore they're quickly fleeting, leaving us believing that life is nothing more than a handful of shallow rewards that leave us empty, disappointed, and frequently angry.

Yet, the immensity of God's blessing are born of an eternal substance. They're cast in "the heavenly realms." His blessings supersede and outclass anything earthly in nature. They are, in fact, other worldly. God's blessing were shaped from the stuff of the eternal which grants them an immense impact entirely unmatched by anything that world can bestow upon us.

A life committed to casting aside the blessings of the world in favor of the eternal blessings born of God is a life rich beyond imagination. Therefore, we might ask, "What are we chasing?" And whatever that is, "Is it worth the chase?" Because if we're chasing things of earth, the pursuit will be one of perpetually cyclical and cynical disappointment.

"The greatest blessings arise when we reject the lesser blessings of men so that we are never dulled to the infinitely greater blessings of God."
~ Craig D. Lounsbrough

Morning Prayer

Dear God:
I know that things disguised as blessings have come my way and will likely come my way again. And I know that I've fallen for them. I admit that their allure was powerful. Their promises were appealing. They were a refreshment to my weary self-esteem, or they were the needed validation for a lagging career, or they dampened the belief that life isn't as dry as I've come to believe it is, or whatever purpose that they served. But they were fleeting. They were this 'fix' that I knew not to be a 'fix.' But, I've fallen for the 'fix' too many times.

I know that the life-sustaining and life-altering blessings come from You...and only You. Everything else is cheap, shallow, and disappointing. I'm tired of settling for that stuff. Compared to Your blessings, the blessings of this world are fraudulent. They're slick imposters attempting to reflect what they are not and what they will never be. Today I refuse those lesser blessings and the people that try to give them to me. Today I commit that I will seek Your blessings only. I will no longer fall for the lesser things that have been such a detriment to my life and seek the greater thing which is You!

I pray all of this in Jesus's Name. Amen

A Thought to Carry with Me Today
"Men seek to imitate the God that they deny in order to convince themselves that they are the god that they are in denial of."
~ Craig D. Lounsbrough

Before this day, I release to God…

_____

_____

_____

_____

_____

Evening Prayer

Dear God:

I recognize that one of the greatest blessings that I experienced today was to reject every blessing that was not from You. Just refusing to accept the lesser things of men so that I don't miss the greater things of God was a blessing all by itself. Dear God, never allow me to settle for anything less than You. I know that I'm prone to do that because those things look good and I'm hungry for them. But they don't satisfy because only You satisfy. Help me to own that thought and never let it go.

Thank You for Your many blessings. Those are gifts. You don't owe me any of that. They are something given to me out of the forever goodness of Your heart. Just knowing that You love me enough to do that is a blessing in itself.

I will settle for nothing less than what You have to give me. I go to bed tonight making that promise to You. Help me to keep it.

I pray all of this in Jesus' Name. Amen.

A Thought to Prepare for Tomorrow
"God eliminates the holes that are continually being dug by the men who are attempting to fill them."
~ Craig D. Lounsbrough

From this day, I release to God...

_____

_____

_____

_____

_____

Day 19

I Am Righteous

*"God made him who had no sin to be
sin for us, so that in him we might become
the righteousness of God."*
~ 2 Corinthians 5:21

We're dirty, or at least that's how we tend to feel at times. And that's not a good feeling. In fact, it's unsettling. Therefore, we're constantly trying to figure out what clean is and how to become whatever that is. We assume that we become clean through some series of actions. So, we work to do the right things. Or we commit to break bad habits. We decide to become charitable in some way that typically eases our guilt more than it actually helps someone else. We backtrack in some broken relationship and attempt to make amends. We do a bunch of stuff to figure out what clean is and become that.

Inherently, these are all good things. They're all things that can bring healing and facilitate a needed restoration. They can repair relationships. They can grant desperately needed hope. They can encourage, lift, restore faith, reinvigorate a passion for life, and bring light to the thickest darkness.

But in the end, they don't expunge the dirt from our lives. And they don't because these things don't make us righteous. Righteousness is a state endowed upon us. It is a gift received. An action imparted. It is not a condition that we create through any series of actions or choices despite how sacrificial or wonderful those might be.

We are scrubbed clean by accepting the sacrificial death of Jesus on our behalf. That's the only way to cleanliness. Our filth was laid on Him "so that in Him we might become the righteousness of God." The stains that defined us. The dirt that shamed us. The grime that repelled us. Gone. Look for it if you will, but with God it is gone!

"The death and resurrection of Jesus didn't scrub us clean. Rather, it purged us of everything filthy so that scrubbing was unnecessary."
~ Craig D. Lounsbrough

Morning Prayer

Dear God:
There are so many times when I thought that I'd cleaned up some area of my life. And I found that there was some relief (and maybe a bit of self-satisfaction) in that for me. But then something happened and I discovered that the dirt never left. It was just as dirty as it'd ever been. I've done all kinds of things to scrub the dirt out of my life. I'm raw from all the scrubbing. And in it all, I know that I'm probably dirtier than I was before I started the scrubbing.

Lord, I'm frustrated, but I'm learning. I'm learning that cleanliness is something that You give to me. It's not something that I create. I can scrub until my hands are raw and my heart is exhausted and yet the dirt remains.

I confess this morning that it is You Who cleanses me. It's acknowledging Your work on the cross on my behalf, and it's accepting that work despite the fact that I don't deserve any of it. It's Your gift that washes me "as white as snow." You and only You hold the soap of the cross. That's the only thing that does it. And beginning today I will live in the righteousness that You give me rather than the righteousness that I try to create.

I pray all of this in Jesus's Name. Amen

A Thought to Carry with Me Today
"To attempt to make myself clean is only to become dirtier in the cleaning."
~ Craig D. Lounsbrough

Before this day, I release to God...

_____

_____

_____

_____

_____

Evening Prayer

Dear God:
I am so glad that You see me through the lens of Jesus work on the cross. And through that lens I am entirely clean. His work on the cross wiped out all of the filth and dirt that I've spent years trying to scrub out of my life. I am so glad that I can actually feel this clean.

But I have to admit that sometimes I don't feel as clean as I know that You've made me. Sometimes I just can't grasp it. I assume that there has to be some dirt hidden somewhere, or I'm in denial of the filth that I'm walking around with. And I know that sometimes I knowingly walk into filthy places that have the same kind of dirt that I've tried to scrub off of myself. But teach me to embrace Your righteousness. Help me to honor it. Live it. And do nothing contrary to the cleansing that You've done in my life.

I pray all of this in Jesus' Name. Amen.

A Thought to Prepare for Tomorrow
"I am confident that God does exactly what He says He does. But I am also sorely aware of the fact that the limitations of my humanity struggle in their ability to embrace the limitlessness of the things He does. Therefore, I am forever thankful that my limits never define His, but that His will never cease to expand mine."
~ Craig D. Lounsbrough

From this day, I release to God...

_____

_____

_____

_____

_____

Day 20

I Am Pure

*"All who have this hope in him purify themselves,
just as he is pure."*
~ *1 John 3:3*

There's no one who doesn't live with regret. We all have a sordid track record of poor choices, damaging decisions, impulsive actions, and things that have left us feeling filthy, marred, and burdened with a regret that we can't shake.

We made choices based on some misdirected passion that led us down roads that we've never been able to walk back up. We've succumbed to lust, or greed, or the lure of material wealth, or the escape of an addiction, or the influence of peers drowning in their own self-destructive choices. And we ended up finding ourselves at the bottom of some cavernous hole with a dirty shovel in sweaty hands wondering why we dug something so deep. And in these places nothing feels pure.

The roads are so long and the holes so deep that we often abandon the idea of purity. It just seems absurdly out of reach. And if somehow we were able to achieve it, we don't feel that we could hold it. That sooner or later we would immerse ourselves in something that would eradicate whatever thin bit of purity we've been able to make room for.

Or we feel that purity is simply not in our nature. There's something in our DNA that predisposes us to this inner ugliness. Yet, John said, "All who have this hope in him [Jesus] purify themselves, just as he is pure." We are given Jesus' purity. Perfect purity. Unconquerable purity. A purity that is undefeatable, pristinely untainted, complete in every way, and sufficiently potent to purge the worst of our impurities right out of us.

*"The worst of us can never stand in
the way of the best of us."*
~ Craig D. Lounsbrough

Morning Prayer

Dear God:
I know that the feeling of being filthy is based on the manner in which I've let these less than admirable things define who I am. I know that when I walk with You, I carry something that no longer exists. I know that the sense of being dirty is only a shadow of the things that once cast that shadow. But because of You those things are gone. Purged and eradicated. I am clean. I am pure. The memory of the shadow is nothing more than that.

I know that I am the biggest obstacle to the things that You want to do in my life. Your purification is complete. Yet, my humanity takes some time to catch up to what You've already completed. Therefore, help me to understand that in You I am not what I used to be. I am a "new creature" who's not used to the newness that has overtaken me. The memories of the past continue to tell me that I am not pure. I am not clean. I am not new. The memories are loud, but Your promises are louder.

This morning help me to walk in Your promises and not rest in my memories. Help me to understand that in You I am pure. I am no longer tainted by a history that no longer defines who I am today. In fact, help me to learn from my history. Help me to grow because of it. Help me to use it for a good that exceeds all of the bad that my history has been. And finally, help any memory of who I was to radically enhance my appreciation of everything that You've allowed me to become.

I pray all of this in Jesus's Name. Amen

A Thought to Carry with Me Today
"One of the greatest ways in which to understand the surpassing ingenuity of God is to hold up who we used to be against who we've become. But possibly the greatest way to see His ingenuity is to allow what He's done to begin revealing the vision of where He's yet to take us. And that is exactly the kind of genius that I will gladly bow before and give the whole of my life to."
~ Craig D. Lounsbrough

Before this day, I release to God...

_____

_____

_____

_____

_____

Evening Prayer

Dear God:
Tonight I claim that in You I am pure. I can't claim that I feel entirely that way. But I know that that's Your truth in me and for me. So, help me to embrace what I can't understand. Help me to understand what I can't yet fathom. Dear God, help me to move beyond the limits that keep me from breaking free to fully embrace what You've done in my life and what You've yet to do. Help me to understand that I am pure.

I want to walk in that understanding. I want to see purity when I look in the mirror even when impurity seems to be all that's staring back at me. I want Your thoughts to be my thoughts so that they might be pure because You are pure. I want to claim that which You have said is rightfully mine to claim. Thank You for making Your purity mine!

I pray all of this in Jesus' Name. Amen.

A Thought to Prepare for Tomorrow

"It is my desperate wish to walk in something bigger than myself simply because to walk in myself is to live a life of small circles and ever-tightening walls. I am dying to walk in something bigger than all of mankind combined because in walking with mankind I am repeatedly faced with the very same circles and exact

same walls. I wish neither of these. Rather, I want to walk in God because in Him there are no circles, walls are unknown, and horizons are the theme of everything He does."
~ Craig D. Lounsbrough

From this day, I release to God...

_____

_____

_____

_____

_____

_____

_____

Day 21

I Am Patient

"Let us not become weary in doing good,
for at the proper time we will reap a harvest
if we do not give up."
~ *Galatians 6:9*

Patience is a virtue. It's just not one of ours...most of the time anyway. Patience is typically based on the expectations that we have placed on something. We have a predetermined sense of how long something should take. How many resources we should have to expend in achieving some goal. How people should act. How complicated a task should or should not be. What should be expected of us and what should not be expected. Patience functions in direct correlation to expectations.

Therefore, if things fall within the tidy parameters of our expectations, patience is not needed simply because things are moving as we have determined they should move. Impatience occurs when something has stepped outside of the parameters of our expectations. The further outside of those parameters something falls, the greater the impatience. The less our ability to pull something back within the parameters we've established, the more the frustration and anger.

The key rests in our expectations. The fact is, our expectations are most often based on how we want the world to operate. We arrogantly superimpose our designs for life upon a far greater design and expect our design to prevail. When it doesn't, our impatience flairs.

God has a "proper time" which is rarely our time. He has a "proper time" that is set to maximize everything that He does. The Bible says that "For everything there is a season." Predetermined. Laid out. Perfect in all aspects. Never early and never late. And if we take the time to understand the seasons that God has fashioned for everything that we do and embrace them as held against our own expectations, patience will not be an issue.

"Patience is acknowledging that the sum
Total of the information needed to move forward
May have not yet come forward in order to
Keep us from moving backward."
~ Craig D. Lounsbrough

Morning Prayer

Dear God:
I already feel impatient and the day has barely begun. I'm already looking ahead and expecting that things will not fit within the neatly designed parameters that I would have them fit within. Whether it's work. A difficult neighbor. My children. Balancing a budget. The timeframe for a project. The things that I hope to accomplish today. I can already feel the impatience roiling within me.

Help me to understand the parameters that You've set for my day...every day and everything in every day. Help me to look to You. If I have any expectations at all, I pray that You would shape them. But I also know that there may be things that You don't want me to have expectations for at all. Maybe Your expectation is that I release these things to You in manner that I place no expectations on them other than "Your will be done."

179

Maybe I need to surrender my expectations to Your perfect timing and the ingenuity of the seasons that You've created. Help me to do these things today.

I pray all of this in Jesus's Name. Amen

A Thought to Carry with Me Today
"My impatience is that utterly stealthy thief that robs me of some of life's greatest moments by whispering that it's 'now or never,' when actually it's 'now will result in never.'"
~ Craig D. Lounsbrough

Before this day, I release to God...

_____

_____

_____

_____

_____

Evening Prayer

Dear God:
I often find myself impatient regarding my impatience. I've had some of that today. And I took some of that out on the people around me. Help me not to do that.

Tonight I commit to understanding Your path. Your seasons. Your timeframes and timelines. Everything that's of You and nothing that's of me. Help me to rid myself of my impatience by walking in Your timing. I ask You to rid me of my inflated sense of urgency. Take away the ticking second hands that aren't counting up to something but always seem to be counting down to something. Take me out of the season that I've created and place me in the season that You're fashioning.

Make me patient. Make me calm. Set my mind at peace because it rests in Yours.

I pray all of this in Jesus' Name. Amen.

A Thought to Prepare for Tomorrow
"Patience is the thing that makes me think
about my choices rather than having my choices
make me think about why I made them."
~ Craig D. Lounsbrough

From this day, I release to God...

_____

_____

_____

_____

_____

_____

_____

Day 22

I Am Kind

"Therefore, as God's chosen people, holy and dearly loved, clothe yourselves with compassion, kindness, humility, gentleness and patience."
~ Colossians 3:12

We often don't feel kind. It's hard to be kind in a world that's rarely kind in return. Being kind means being vulnerable. It means setting a defensive stance aside and leaning into something that might lean back in a less than kind way. It means risking for little return.

We get jaded. We come to assume that kindness really doesn't get us all that far. It tends to set us up for painful freefalls and hard landings. And even if something good might eventually arise out of being kind, at some point we seem to get tapped out and just don't have it within us to be kind anymore. Kindness has killed us.

We often conceptualize kindness in respect to the risk we take in being kind and the vulnerability that it creates for us rather than understanding the impact that it has on others. Yes, we're probably going to get wounded. Rejection is possible, even likely in many situations. Exhibiting "compassion, kindness, humility, gentleness and patience" is risky as are all great things. But too often we have weighed these things in relation to the cost that we incur versus the impact on others.

God knows that being kind can result in difficult things. Out of an eternal kindness God sent His Son to trade His life for ours. And yes, His kindness was betrayed. Brutally. But if we focus on the brutality itself and miss the billions of lives utterly transformed by that single act of kindness we will have missed the power of kindness in action.

Kindness is intentional. It is potent. It's transformational. It can be strengthened in the wounding. And what gives it power is the selflessness with which it is delivered.

> *"When it comes to killing people, my weapon*
> *of choice is kindness."*
> *~ Craig D. Lounsbrough*

Morning Prayer

Dear God:
I'm not very kind a lot of the time. Really, I'm more edgy most of the time. Kindness takes a lot of energy. Most of the time it's not my preference. I'd rather lash out, or put someone in their place, or shun them altogether. Often those are my preferences because they're easy, they're quick, and they push irritating people away.

But I know that You want to clothe me with "compassion, kindness, humility, gentleness and patience." And I want to be clothed in those things because I know that there's nothing better to be clothed in. Dear God, I know that I'm not always receptive to that kind of stuff. I know that I can be stubborn. But I also know that what You can do through me when I'm wearing these things is beyond anything that I can imagine.

And so today, I'm going to work on wearing these as best I can. I might wear some better than others. Some might seem more of a fit than others. But I will wear them because not to is to live a diminished life and leave diminished people behind me in the living. And that is not how I want to live. So, clothe me today and every day.

I pray all of this in Jesus's Name. Amen

A Thought to Carry with Me Today
"What I wear on the outside is determined by what resides on the inside. And it is my goal to wear kindness not because it looks good on me, but because it resides within me."
~ Craig D. Lounsbrough

Before this day, I release to God...

_____

_____

_____

_____

_____

_____

_____

_____

Evening Prayer

Dear God:
I thank you that You are kind. You are kind in ways that stun me. You are kind when there is every reason not to be kind. Kindness is Your choice. It's Your nature. Your kindness is not permissive or naïve. It's never caused You to turn a blind eye to everything that's not kind. It's a bold kindness that's fully aware of the wickedness that You deliver that kindness into. You grant mankind permission to refuse, ignore, slander, and reject Your kindness. It can be shunned and ridiculed, and You know that it will be. But You give it anyway.

And I believe that You repeatedly offer it up for the simple reason that the power of kindness can handily overcome the greatest wickedness. Kindness is not soft. Rather, it's penetrating. It is not passive. Rather, it's brazen. It changes what everything else fails to change. And tonight I want You to deliver that kindness through me. Clothe me in it. I want to be a conduit of kindness…Your kindness.

I pray all of this in Jesus' Name. Amen.

A Thought to Prepare for Tomorrow
"Kindness is the lesser side of ourselves subjugated to something greater than ourselves."
~ Craig D. Lounsbrough

From this day, I release to God...

_____

_____

_____

_____

_____

_____

_____

_____

Day 23

I Am Covered in God's Armor

"Finally, be strong in the Lord and in his mighty power. Put on the full armor of God, so that you can take your stand against the devil's schemes."
~ Ephesians 6:10

Security seems more the illusion that we craft to offset our fears. Something suddenly swerves into our lives and we're faced with the truth that we're desperately vulnerable. Hopes that appeared firmly grounded are rocked to rubble. Finances that seemed safeguarded burst into a fiscal inferno. Relationships bonded strong by the steeled cords of time are ripped apart as frayed threads. Friends disappear as if they had never been. An addiction throws a career into a deathly freefall. A car accident steals a life. A diagnosis is terminal. The illusion of security falls to reality every day.

We seem to stand stripped before a world that's brutally insensitive to whoever it crushes in its mad advance to nowhere. Sometimes everything appears to be a risk. There's nothing that's firm or safe. There's no shield, no barrier, no place of refuge, and no strong tower. It's a life of risk infused with an ever-accelerating fear.

Yet we have been gifted the "full armor of God." And this armor is not forged to repel the simplistic and impotent attacks of men, for men can forge that kind of armor. Rather, it's forged to "stand against the devil's schemes." It's forged to be invincible. Impermeable. Indestructible. Entirely suited to equip anyone who dares to don it as a relentless victor moving out in armor unmatched.

Wearing the armor will demand obedience to it. It will require a constant awareness of its attributes, an ever-increasing proficiency in the use of its various parts, and an unending respect for what each part does. God's armor takes our frailty and encases that frailty in victory unfolding and defeat defeated.

"It doesn't matter what's coming at us. God defeated it before it ever left wherever it was coming from."
~ Craig D. Lounsbrough

Morning Prayer

Dear God:
Life seems to fight my attempts to live it. Life seems to want me to be beaten before I have any chance to enrich the life that's out to beat me. It all seems to be an uphill battle for no good reason other than there's some sort of brutality built into it all. It's a battle for no other reason than Satan is dead-set upon my destruction, even if the illusion of achievement helps him achieve that destruction.

You know my wounds. In fact, You know them better than I do. Those wounds tell me that I'm not invincible, even at those times when I thought I was. They tell me that the world isn't interested in my wounds other than causing them. The more I have, the more I become convinced that I will forever live a defeated life.

But the effect of my wounds is the righteous anger that they create for me. The more the wounds, the more committed I become to beating that which has been wounding me. My wounds are not the end of my story.

Rather, I want them to be the beginning of Your story in me. And so, today I put on Your armor, because wearing that armor shifts the battlefield, tilts the battle itself, and changes my story. So today, I put on this armor and I walk in it.

I pray all of this in Jesus's Name. Amen

A Thought to Carry With Me Today

"Being alert is not to vigilantly stand on tip-toe in order to scan some distant horizon out of the fear of some approaching enemy. Quite the opposite. It is falling to our knees knowing that God is already out on that horizon and that He thwarted the enemy long before they ever reached it."
~ Craig D. Lounsbrough

Before this day, I release to God...

_____

_____

_____

_____

_____

_____

_____

_____

_____

Evening Prayer

Dear God:
I wore the armor today. I didn't necessarily wear it well, but I wore it. I found myself with a wavering faith in its invincibility, hesitation regarding my ability to effectively utilize it, and at times I doubted its existence altogether. Even though I wore it, I found myself frightened to step into situations that this armor would have completely protected me from. The armor is invincible, but my faith in it is not.

Thank You for the armor. Thank You that You have gifted it to me. Help me to better understand it. Help me to better wear it. Help me to have faith in its design. And help me to impact the battles that surround me by utilizing this armor to the fullest extent for which You created it and intended it.

I pray all of this in Jesus' Name. Amen.

A Thought to Prepare for Tomorrow
"Prayer inserts me into the middle of any
battlefield regardless of how gruesome or bloodied.
And in the carnage of whatever that battle might be,
it allows me to deliver a force greater than
any raging on that field."
~ Craig D. Lounsbrough

Taking It to Our Knees

From this day, I release to God...

_____

_____

_____

_____

_____

_____

_____

_____

_____

Day 24

I Am Wrapped in God's Arms

"You have been a refuge for the poor, a refuge for the needy in their distress, a shelter from the storm and a shade from the heat."
~ *Isaiah 25:4*

We want the reassurance of relationship. Somehow being connected to someone makes us bigger than the sum total of who we both are. There's a camaraderie of necessity in this existence of ours. As John Donne famously said, "No man is an island." We are not created to be isolate entities forging some isolated path through the turbulence of the storm or the moments of elation. Those times are enriched by partnership and diminished by its absence.

Yet we've been burnt by people. In whatever form that happened, we've been burnt. And as the saying goes, "Once burnt, twice smart." We want the reassurance of relationship, but we fear the risk that works against that reassurance. A spouse left. A child walked away. A business partner undercut us. A parent abandoned us for another marriage and a different family. A friend found the commitment of a friendship an inconvenience as held against personal agendas. Yes, we want the reassurance of relationship, but we fear the risk that works against that reassurance.

Yet, God is described as a refuge, a shelter, and shade. In Psalm 18 He is referred to as our strength, our rock, our fortress, our deliverer, our shield, and our salvation. The connotation is one of perfect security. Absolute protection. Impenetrable. Perfectly reliable regardless of what comes against us. We want the reassurance of relationship. And God grants us that with a reliable protection that renders risk emptied of risk.

*"I can staunchly reject the notion that I
Was created to live in relationship with God. But
should I do that, I will be unable to reject all of the
consequences for which I was not created."*
~ Craig D. Lounsbrough

Morning Prayer

Dear God:
I'm done living alone. I mean, I'm around people, but I'm alone while being around them. I don't trust myself to them. I can state all of the reasons why I don't trust them. Some of those are valid, and some are not. Some are real, and some are things that I've allowed my imagination to inflate. But despite all of that I'm done living alone.

Beginning today I claim You as my refuge, my shelter, my shade, my strength, my rock, my fortress, my deliverer, my shield, and my salvation. I claim You as all of those things. I claim those in every area of my life. In everything that I do and in everyone I encounter. In every success and every failure I claim You as the perfect security that stands immovable against all of life's insecurities.

And as I rest in these things that You have become in my life, I pray for the courage and the confidence to reach out into all of the many things are not those things. May the fear of the world around me and the people that inhabit that world be pressed aside as I rest in Who You are to me. May I restlessly forge into a world that needs to witness who and what a person can be who rests in Who You are.

I pray all of this in Jesus's Name. Amen

A Thought to Carry With Me Today
"There are many who don't believe in God. But I would imagine that every one of them had more than one moment where they wished they believed."
~ Craig D. Lounsbrough

Before this day, I release to God...

_____

_____

_____

_____

_____

Evening Prayer

Dear God:
Tonight I claim You as my refuge, my shelter, my shade, my strength, my rock, my fortress, my deliverer, my shield, and my salvation. I claim You as all of those things as I end my day. And I claim an immovable confidence in each one of these. I claim as mine the immense power that is manifest when all of them are brought to bear in and on my life.

197

Craig D. Lounsbrough

Tonight I once again reassert my commitment to walk in these truths. I commit to walking into a world that is tenuous, unsafe, dark, and set on hurting those who stand for You. I know that the things that You provide grant me a security and a safety more than sufficiently formidable to face that which is tenuous, unsafe, dark, and set on hurting those who love You. In You, I am eternally outside of their reach. And so tonight, I claim them, I embrace them, I walk in them, and I commit to resting in the walking.

I pray all of this in Jesus' Name. Amen.

A Thought to Prepare for Tomorrow
"These are the times when our faith is not just an idea or a concept that we throw around. It's something that has to actually be lived out. We must rise to what we say we believe. And when we do, God rises with us. He walks alongside us. The exercise of our faith never comes back empty."
~ Craig D. Lounsbrough

From this day, I release to God...

_____
_____
_____
_____
_____

Day 25

I Am Heard

*"I love the LORD, for he heard my voice; he heard my
cry for mercy. Because he turned his ear to me, I will
call on him as long as I live."*
~ Psalm 116:1-2

Listening is based on the value that something or someone holds for us. If there's some degree of value assigned to a person, or a cause, or some philosophy, we will tend to listen to it. The greater the value that we place on something, the more we listen. Conversely, if we've assigned no value to whatever these things might be, we don't listen. Essentially, there's no pay-off in listening.

We live in a world where individuals are prone to ascribe a certain value to themselves. Often that self-assigned value surpasses the value that they ascribe to others. In this self-determined pecking order, we often find ourselves possessing insufficient value as held against their self-assigned value. Therefore, their assessments frequently marginalize our voice and relegate us to the sphere of the irrelevant.

And in this punishing dynamic, the longing to be heard remains a longing. It's not about having someone agree with our opinions or embrace our perspectives. It's about the fact that someone cared enough to stop, bring their lives to a halt on our behalf, and just listen. Listening says that we matter. That our existence is actually worthwhile. And we want to be worthwhile.

We must remember that God puts no value on status. The Bible says that **"People look at the outward appearance, but the LORD looks at the heart."** He puts value on you. You are never relegated to the sphere of the irrelevant by the fact that He is God and you are not. Your voice is never assessed by any other value than it is the voice that He is longing to hear. Yes, God listens. Always. Every time. To everything.

"At those times when the loneliness has gone on for so long that we have little alternative than to believe that loneliness is the single story that life has penned for us and that there is no other story...at those times we wonder if anyone is listening. And at those times, we would be wise to remember that God is listening to our wondering."
~ Craig D. Lounsbrough

Morning Prayer

Dear God:

I'm praying this morning because I have faith that You're listening. I know that the world that I will be walking into this morning won't be listening. Not today. Not tomorrow. It might pause and give me a bit of attention here and there, but if what I say doesn't serve its agenda or mesh with its preferences it's unlikely to really listen.

However, You listen. And You hear. You actually hear. These words of mine don't fade into the 'nothing' that so many of my other words appear to fade into. You turn and You listen. But far more than that, You take all of these words of mine into account. As awkward as they might be sometimes, You deem them as precious. Important. Priceless. You remember them, and then You actually act on them. And while the world often turns a deaf ear to me, You press that world aside, You

Craig D. Lounsbrough

sit next to me, You turn to me, and You listen. You listen. And if I can just grasp the magnitude and immense wonder of that single truth, the world can ignore me for the rest of my life because I have a God Who never will. So, thank you for listening…today and every day.

I pray all of this in Jesus's Name. Amen

A Thought to Carry With Me Today
"In the Bible God says, 'Then you will call on me and come and pray to me, and I will listen to you.' God will listen. Not out of obligation. Not because you are a project. Not because you are a charity case. Not because God is checking a box. There's none of that. The fact is, He created us to be heard by Him. Therefore, He can do nothing other than listen to us."
~ Craig D. Lounsbrough

Before this day, I release to God…

_____

_____

_____

_____

_____

_____

Evening Prayer

Dear God:
I know that You listened to me today. When I prayed. When my heart ached. When it was deluged with joy. Whatever place I was in, You listened. There was never a moment when You were so distant or preoccupied that You had to trade time with me for something else. There was never a second where You tired of me or ceased longing to hear my voice. You made hearing me a priority. You made me feel that somewhere within me there lays a person of great value, even though I frequently doubt that person's existence.

But God, I want to listen to You as well. Help me to hear Your voice. Help me to always create a space for Your words. Help me to bring my life to a halt, press aside the earsplitting voices of a world that never shuts up, and just listen to You. For Your voice is the One that I want to hear above any other voice that I could ever listen to. Help me to hear You.

I pray all of this in Jesus' Name. Amen.

A Thought to Prepare for Tomorrow
"Suddenly someone stops long enough to listen. And in that simple action, some marginalized person finally realizes that they actually have a story to tell and that it's worth the telling. Therefore, I make it a point to stop rather frequently."
~ Craig D. Lounsbrough

From this day, I release to God...

_____

_____

_____

_____

_____

_____

_____

_____

Day 26

I Am Enough

*"Not that we are competent in
ourselves to claim anything for ourselves,
but our competence comes from God."*
~ 2 Corinthians 3:5

We are deficit focused. We're prone to be on some sort of mad hunt where we're constantly tracking down our deficits. These deficits are often defined by this elusive process of hitting some societal target that is always moving based on any number of trending trends, or what might be deemed to be vogue at any given moment. Whether they're real, imagined, or exaggerated, we rigorously list these deficits in some dark and ever-lengthening column of our lives. This exacting endeavor readily presses any positives aside into the oblivion of the ignored.

This deficit-focused mentality is nothing more than a race within which we fall further and further behind. After years of expending the best of ourselves and our resources in this degenerative pursuit, the failure of our efforts convinces that we are not enough. Defeated by the best of our efforts, our sense of hopelessness closes in on us.

Paul says, we "are complete through [our] union with Christ." Another translation puts it as we "have been brought to fullness." Complete. Entirely intact. All of which is achieved through our relationship with Christ. The Psalmist confidently says that we are "fearfully and wonderfully made." We are enough. But enough is even insufficient, for God has made us 'more' than enough. His design as manifest in us exceeds any concept of 'enough.' There is an essence about us, something formed and fashioned within us that exceeds the weak rubrics that we apply to ourselves. We are 'enough' in a way that is more than enough.

*"God is confident enough in me to be all
things confident for me."*
~ Craig D. Lounsbrough

Morning Prayer

Dear God:
I like to pretend that I'm enough. I put on a pretty good
show and I've fooled a lot of people. But in those lonely
moments like this one, when I've left the games at the
door of my life and I sit in honest reflection, I don't feel
that I am enough.

And although I don't totally understand it, I know that
my efforts are never going to be enough to make me
feel like I'm enough. And yet, that's the very stuff that
I chase. That's where I end up expending my life.
Inevitably I come to some place of utter exhaustion
finally understanding that I'm not good enough to make
myself good enough. But sooner or later I press that
reality aside because I'm so desperate to be enough.
And in time, I'm right back to doing all of the things
that have repeatedly failed to make me feel that I'm
enough of whatever it is that I need to be enough of.

I confess this morning that You say that I'm enough.
I'm sufficient as I am. It's all good. The Bible is full of
those statements. You've declared my worth over and
over. And I know that You did that to pound that truth
into my head because it runs against everything that I
believe about myself. I know that I need some
pounding. But today I'm going to work on believing it.

207

More than that, I'm going to act on even though I might not feel it. Thank You that I'm enough. Help me to act on that truth.

I pray all of this in Jesus' Name. Amen.

A Thought to Carry with Me Today

"Possibly the greatest failure of all is to assert that our failures declare our value as being the same as that which we continue to fail at."
~ Craig D. Lounsbrough

Before this day, I release to God...

_____

_____

_____

_____

Evening Prayer

Dear God:
The world wasn't very affirming today. But, I don't suppose that I should expect it to be. I have to stop letting the opinions and evaluations that the world levies upon me be the things that define me. The world defines me in a way that meets its own objectives, therefore it will never be a reflection of who I am. Rather, it will be a reflection of what the world wants me to be. And I have no interest in that.

You say that I am enough. Yet, what You're really declaring is that I'm 'more' than enough. You made me more than enough. You made me better than better. You were serious when You designed me. And You were serious when You sent Your Son so that that design could be unleashed in all of its brilliance. All of that makes me more than enough for today, tomorrow, and eternity itself.

Tonight I ask You to cement these truths in my head and my heart. Root them deeply within me to the point that any notion of worthlessness finds no place to take root. I thank You that You crafted me as someone who is (and will always be) more than enough.

I pray all of this in Jesus' Name. Amen.

A Thought to Prepare for Tomorrow
"God is precise, deliberate and intentional. Therefore, everything He created held sufficient value for Him to create it. And of all things, that means you."
~ Craig D. Lounsbrough

From this day, I release to God…

_____

_____

_____

_____

Day 27

I Am Not Alone

"Be strong and courageous. Do not be afraid or terrified because of them, for the LORD your God goes with you; he will never leave you nor forsake you."
~ Deuteronomy 31:6

There's the feeling of loneliness. But that feeling embodies many things that define that feeling and give it life. We are often alone in facing a loss, dealing with an addiction, navigating the political terrain of a job, managing a difficult neighbor, confronting a financial crisis, or just getting ourselves out of bed. Loneliness is not just a feeling. Rather, it is the manifestation of a number of challenges that life sideswipes us with.

Loneliness itself doesn't invite anyone into our circumstances. Rather, it's isolating. By its very nature it's confining. The pattern that it perpetuates keeps us isolated. In essence, loneliness multiplies loneliness by keeping it lonely.

Additionally, the world is often not a friendly place. It's a place of suspicion and mutual distrust. Therefore, it does little to remediate loneliness. The world separates through fear, greed, intimidation, jealous rivalry, the creation of conflicting agendas, and more.

Yet, God "will never leave you nor forsake you." He "goes with you." There's a promised camaraderie. A companionship that never misses a moment or fails to walk in lockstep with us. That's quite a promise. At times, that may seem to be an impossible promise that's more the stuff of muse or some nice ideal rather than a sustainable reality. Yet, it's a promise. And it's repeated over and over. It never fails, is never lacking, never sticks with us out of pity or personal agenda and is unphased by how dark the path might become or how massive the challenges might be. You are never alone…ever.

"The battle is never fought alone even though we might feel alone in the fight, for with God the feeling of being alone never supersedes the fact of His presence."
~ *Craig D. Lounsbrough*

Morning Prayer

Dear God:
I sit here thinking about what lies in front of me today. There will be demands. There will be obstacles and challenges. There will be a time where I will be in the company of people, at other times when the company of people will be absent, and yet other times when I will be alone in the company of people. I know that I will yearn for someone to share my moments with me and I will find none that are willing or able to do so. I will be isolated at some point in my day wondering how a world so full of people could be so full of emptiness.
You say that You "hem me in behind and before." So, whether I look forward or backward, You are there. If I step into the future or work to heal from the past, You are there. Your presence is inclusive. Total. Comprehensive. You know where I've been, and You know where I'm going. And You are in both places at the same time all of the time.

So today, if I face a loss, or an addiction, or if I have to navigate the political terrain of my job, or manage a difficult neighbor, or confront a financial crisis, or just get myself out of bed, You are there. Every time at all times. Today I claim that I am not alone. And I claim that I will never be alone. Thank You for that truth today and every day!

I pray all of this in Jesus's Name. Amen.

A Thought to Carry with Me Today
"Being alone is that sense of abject isolation in the midst of our most grievous pain. Yet, if the former is swept away by the presence of God, then the latter stands ready to be healed by the hand of God."
~ Craig D. Lounsbrough

Before this day, I release to God...

_____

_____

_____

_____

Evening Prayer

Dear God:
I know that You will sit by my bedside tonight. And I know that You will walk with me tomorrow. You surround me on all sides. You are healing my yesterday and You are already out in my tomorrow preparing it for my arrival. And You are doing all of that while You're sitting with me right here, right now.

213

I know that I can pray these things. And I believe them with what little bit of faith that I have. But I'm asking You to increase my faith. I'm asking You to make this truth more real for me than I can imagine sitting here right now. Help me to know that You're there. Help me to hear Your voice. Sense Your steps next to mine. Feel Your arms around me. And be lost in the fact that You are not only here right now, but that You will never be any other place than at my side. I claim that I am not alone. And I declare tonight that I will never be alone. Thank You for loving me enough to walk with me always.

I pray all of this in Jesus' Name. Amen.

A Thought to Prepare for Tomorrow
"Should all the hordes of mankind assemble as one and bring the full force of their numbers against us, we must remember that one man standing alone with God remains an immovable majority."
~ Craig D. Lounsbrough

From this day, I release to God...

_____

_____

_____

_____

_____

Day 28

I Am Healed

*"He himself bore our sins in his body on the cross,
so that we might die to sins and live for righteousness;
by his wounds you have been healed."*
~ *1 Peter 2:24*

The walking wounded are among us because they are all of us. No one is without wounds. No one walks free of lacerations. We all have a limp, or a contusion, or a fracture. We all have something broken, or something that's about to be broken, or something's that's about to be broken again. The wounded are as close as ourselves.

The wounds seem to layer themselves upon each other. A spouse leaves. A job goes sideways. The diagnosis is terminal. A parent passes. The addiction grows and our ability to fight it shrinks. A child falls to the lies of culture, and hope falls to the ever-darkening propaganda that engulfs the culture. The wounds multiply, the bleeding never stops, and the ability to heal is sabotaged by whatever's waiting in the wings this time. Our lives move from being wounded, to healing, to being wounded again.

Healing in a wounding world seems a terrible oxymoron that both teases us with hope and disappoints us with reality. Yet disappointment falls to hope because, "He Himself bore our sins in His body on the cross." And because God made that utterly astonishing decision, "by His wounds you have been healed." It is by "His wounds" because the wounding of the world cannot be healed by the world. The worlds' ability to inflict pain will always exceed its ability to heal it. And therefore we must have something greater than the world to do that. And that greater thing was the Son of Man engaging in a transaction so brutal (but so comprehensive because of its brutality) that nothing stands outside of its power and effect. We are healed, despite the gravity of the wound and the persistence of a world determined to wound us again. We are the walking wounded who are now running healed.

> *"I am left with no alternative than to look beyond the efforts of men, for efforts of those sort leave cities flattened, nations teetering, and lives crushed. Instead, I must shift the whole of my gaze to the God who tenderly kneels in the midst of this unimaginable carnage and effortlessly makes the healing imaginable."*
> ~ *Craig D. Lounsbrough*

Morning Prayer

Dear God:

I wake up to pain. My wounds greet me every morning, reminding me that my existence is less about healing those wounds and more about surrendering to them. They arrogantly assume a place in my life that has come to define my life, diminish my existence, and shape my future. And I sit here haunted by the wounds that seem to taunt me without end. Worse yet, I barely roll out of bed before I'm casting an anxious eye on the coming day as I am certain that it will show up with something that's going to wound me yet again.

This is not how You want me to live. This is not Your intent. This is not Your design. Instead, this is Your design perverted by mankind's sin. And I am thankful

Craig D. Lounsbrough

that You have not (and will not) stand for such a revolting perversion. Such was Your hatred of this that it drove You to send Your Son to be wounded in a manner so unimaginably brutal that my wounds would be healed by His. You provided the perfect cure. The total cure. The forever cure. And today I embrace that cure and I bring it to bear on my every wound.

I pray all of this in Jesus's Name. Amen.

A Thought to Carry with Me Today
"I believe that the healing for everything that's ever been broken in my life was on its way long before the brokenness thought that it had its way."
~ Craig D. Lounsbrough

Before this day, I release to God...

_____
_____
_____
_____
_____
_____
_____
_____
_____

Evening Prayer

Dear God:

You know where I'm bruised tonight. You know my every wound...perfectly. Even the ones that I'm not aware of. And You hold the solution to every one of them. No wound that I will ever have is beyond the healing that You can bring to it. I might sit swallowed up in some sort of pain that I find unbearable and beyond any cure, but You stand ready to say, "Be healed," despite how much of me this pain might have swallowed me up.

And that healing is never some disappointing prescription that numbs but does not heal. It's never passive, or shallow, or a victim of the wound that it seeks to heal. It's what every other solution is not and never will be. It's born of Your Son's death on the cross. That's strong medicine. Therefore, that healing is total in every respect. Complete in every way. Comprehensive beyond comprehension. And tonight I claim that healing. Whether it's immediate, or whether it will be best accomplished over time, or whether it will be left because there's something in the pain that's more precious than the pain itself. Whatever the case might be, I claim a healing tonight. And I claim it with thanks.

I pray all of this in Jesus' Name. Amen.

Craig D. Lounsbrough

A Thought to Prepare for Tomorrow
"God's trying to get your attention in order to heal the pain that's got your attention."
~ Craig D. Lounsbrough

From this day, I release to God...

_____

_____

_____

_____

_____

_____

_____

_____

_____

Day 29

I Am Accepted

"Accept one another, then, just as Christ accepted you, in order to bring praise to God."
~ *Romans 15:7*

We live in a world that accepts us based on conditions. And those conditions are not something that we set. We have to deny who we are and betray our inner core in order to obtain the acceptance that we are desperate to have. It is an exercise of troubling compromise, disturbing adherence, soul-suffocating obedience, and the abandonment of everything that we thought we would never abandon. And once we are stripped by this forced conforming, we are accepted on the condition that more stripping continue.

Acceptance is conditional. It empties us of ourselves and forces us to mimic who or what we seek acceptance from. In that sense it's rejection of the greatest kind. It's a declaration that we are only good enough if we betray ourselves in favor of everything that is not us. It's a revision that demands the exclusion of who we are in the revising. It's contingent upon the abandonment of self which is a betrayal of our very existence.

Yet we seek unconditional acceptance. We seek someone who is willing to take us as we are; as raw, as unappealing, as broken, and as dull as we might be. And in just such a relationship it is our hope that the rejection of our essence will finally be reversed by the cultivation of it. We want someone to cherish who we are with an eye toward nurturing that essence without constraint, condition, purposeless agenda, or fear.

"Christ accepted you" as you are right now. As raw, as unappealing, as broken, or as dull as we might be. His acceptance is total, pure, uncompromising, and entirely engulfed by a vision that is sold out to the maximization your every asset.

"Our true selves accepted, cultivated, and unleashed is immense. But what is infinitely greater than all of these is the loss that will occur if none of these happen."
~ Craig D. Lounsbrough

Morning Prayer

Dear God:
I want to start my day immersed in Your acceptance of me. Right now I want to be awash in that feeling. You chose me "before the creation of the world." Before anything existed You chose me. You accepted me before I ever felt the need to be accepted. Before I was lonely. Before the world rejected me in all of the ways that it's rejected me. You chose me before I was ever ridiculed, abandoned, betrayed, and cast aside in favor of so many lesser things. I was chosen by You before I was ever rejected by the world.

I want to thank You for that. I want to thank You because in too many instances I have not returned the favor. I have demanded that You be something that You're not. I have demanded that You adhere to my whims, bend to my preferences, and accommodate my greed. And yet, You have never done that to me. Ever. Thank You for accepting me all of the many times that I refused to accept You. Thank You that You have declared me worthy even when I have not declared You as such.

I pray all of this in Jesus's Name. Amen.

A Thought to Carry with Me Today
"I take my cues from the world around me and carefully paint a self-portrait that the world can't help but accept. However, I would be much wiser to put down all such artistic notions and hold up the portrait of me painted by God simply because that is a picture at which the world can't help but marvel."
~ Craig D. Lounsbrough

Before this day, I release to God...

_____

_____

_____

_____

Evening Prayer

Dear God:
I know that You accept me despite many of the choices that I made today. And right now I confess those choices. Many of them didn't enhance my life. Most of them won't do what others promised they would do or what I promised they would do. They were one of my many bad moments. And I ask You to forgive me of those.

But I know that You accept me even when I'm not at my best, which is most of the time. You stand by me at the moments that I would not stand by me. You are relentlessly loyal and always committed. Thank You for accepting me in a way that I don't even accept me. And thank You for accepting me even when I don't accept You. I know that I can't earn Your acceptance. I know that it's a gift that the best of myself could never possibly hope to earn and the worst of myself never ceases to abuse. And because of these things, help me to act in accordance with Your acceptance in a way that brings You joy and brings me closer to You.

I pray all of this in Jesus' Name. Amen.

A Thought to Prepare for Tomorrow
"God has gifted us with both the right and
the privilege of accepting Him or rejecting Him.
And the immensity of the distance that lays between
the outcomes of those two choices is greater by
far than any other choice that any human
being will ever make."
~ Craig D. Lounsbrough

From this day, I release to God...

_____

_____

_____

_____

Day 30

I Have a Future

> " 'For I know the plans I have for you,' declares
> the LORD, 'plans to prosper you and not to harm you,
> plans to give you hope and a future.' "
> ~ Jeremiah 29:11

Too often the future is built on the doubts of today. We live in troubling times. Our culture is immersed in philosophies that are void of wisdom and permeated with the rot of greed. Nation's teeter. Wars rage. Economies flounder. Identities fall prey to scandalous revisions. Suicides are commonplace. Hope is elusive. And if we are able to craft some vision of the future from the darkness of these realities, it's bleak.

But God says, "I know the plans that I have for you." He has a plan. An invincible plan. A plan that is not intimidated by teetering nations, raging wars, floundering economies, forfeited identities, suicides, or elusive hope. A plan that is never fazed by today. A plan that our tomorrow's will be entirely subjected to. A plan that is impervious to all the combined schemes of men in whatever place or time that those schemes might be hurled against us. The plans that He has for us will always supersede the constraints of our existence and the impact of the people who share that existence with us.

The road of tomorrow is paved by the decisions of today. You are part of paving those roads. You will walk some of them. Some you won't, but others will. The beauty of God's plan is such that you have been granted an indispensable role in shaping both the nature of this day and the road it will pave for tomorrow, whether you will be the one to walk that road or whether you are paving it for others who will walk it without you. Either way, God says, "...I know the plans

I have for you." Astonishing plans. Phenomenal roads. Nothing short of a "hope and a future."

> *"Might we remember what God has*
> *saved us from in the past, so that we might*
> *be saved from our fear of the future."*
> *~ Craig D. Lounsbrough*

Morning Prayer

Dear God:
I can't see into today from where I'm at this morning. Sure, I can guess at what's going to happen. I have a basic idea and today will likely head somewhere in that direction. But that's all a guess. Not a certainty. And I know that if today is a guess, tomorrow is even more of a guess, much less next month or next year. Uncertainty is a cruel thing and it sits with me every day.

But my future doesn't rest in uncertainty. It doesn't rest in what the world does or what the world is. My future rests in You. You've got it planned out. Every detail. Every second. Every twist and every turn in every road that I am privileged to help pave. You've laid it out in front of me. And not only is it out there in front of me, it's precisely laid out. It's ingenious and it's Your gift to me. You knew that future before it ever came to be. And You knew the role that You would have me play in it before there was ever a role to play or a future to play it in. And so today, I trust in that future. I know that things will come my way today. I know that the news will likely be bleak. And I know that those around

228

me will preach hopelessness from dark pulpits of fear. Known or unknown, I will get sideswiped by these things. But I declare today that You know the plans that You have for me and that You intend to work them out in both the best and the worst of the day to come.

I pray all of this in Jesus's Name. Amen.

A Thought to Carry With Me Today

"How do I plan a future when my past is fuzzy, I'm uncertain about today, and the best I can do is to hazard a 'best-guess' about tomorrow? With God, the answer rests not in creating a plan but discovering one."
~ Craig D. Lounsbrough

Before this day, I release to God...

_____

_____

_____

_____

Evening Prayer

Dear God:
I thank You that I can go to bed knowing that there will be a tomorrow beyond every tomorrow. The future is set. It's determined. It's solid. It's reliable. And You've outlined a specific role that I will play in that future.

That role is shaped to that future, and that future is shaped to that role. And I know that it's not just shaped to navigate whatever the future will be. It's shaped to pierce it, penetrate it, and transform it.

Thank You that You've gifted me with a future. But more than that, thank You that You have gifted me with an indispensable role in that future. I pray that I can live that role out fully, completely, without compromise, void of any fearful resignation, and in exactly the manner in which You planned it. Thank You that an eternity of tomorrow's is set before me and that there is both a place and a role for me in every one of them!

I pray all of this in Jesus' Name. Amen.

A Thought to Prepare for Tomorrow
"I took a walk this morning. And as I did, I wished that an awakening world would see opportunities in this day that it did not see when it went to bed last night. And I further wished that when it went to bed at the close of this day, it did so with enough hope for a thousand mornings of opportunity."
~ Craig D. Lounsbrough

From this day, I release to God...

_____

_____

_____

_____

Day 31

I Am at Peace

"Do not be anxious about anything, but in every situation, by prayer and petition, with thanksgiving, present your requests to God. And the peace of God, which transcends all understanding, will guard your hearts and your minds in Christ Jesus."
~ Philippians 4:6-7

Peace is the anthesis of our existence, yet our soul begs for it. We strive for peace, but we create chaos in the striving. We pray for calm, but our decisions result in conflict. We seize hastily crafted philosophies and throw them against the rising anarchy, only to add yet another dysfunctional layer to the bedlam. We beg for peace, but we work against the very thing that we beg for.

Our efforts at achieving peace are undercut by self-serving agendas, repealed by our fears, capsized by the foolishness of our contrived wisdom, and annulled by the vagrant philosophies that have captured our fancy. In our pursuit of peace we become authors of chaos, perpetuators of conflict, and enablers of anarchy. The peace that we seek is at ever-further distances from us as we work against it thinking that we're working for it. We are not authors of peace. Rather, we are scribblers of bedlam.

Pure, undiluted, and invincible peace can only thrive in a place where the things that would destroy it are themselves destroyed. We are entirely defenseless before such things. But God is defenseless before nothing. He is perfect peace because these things are perfectly absent in Him. His peace is invincible because He is invincible. He grants us the "peace that passes all understanding" because Who He is eclipses our understanding. It is the peace that we will never understand, but it is the peace that God grants us the privileging of standing under. This is the peace of all peace.

*"If you take stock of the world you will realize
that the peace of the world is 'peace' in name only,
where real peace rests in Jesus' name only."*
~ Craig D. Lounsbrough

Morning Prayer

Dear God:

I wish I could say that I was at peace this morning, but I am not. I know that I've had some moments where I was more at peace than at other moments, but even then it seemed to slip away before I had any real chance to sit with it. I confess to You that I'm never at peace in a way that has that absolute sense of calm about it. That kind of peace is more a dream that I'm constantly working to conjure up, rather than a reality that I actually live in.

Peace seems impossible, at least real peace. The world that I live in doesn't have a whole lot of peace in it. It seems that everything works against any kind of peace. We've created a world that's anything but peaceful because what we've created has been created in rebellion against the only Person Who's got that kind of peace to give.

But I'm coming to You and I'm asking You to bring that peace into my life. Help me to make certain that I don't do what the world's done and therefore destroy the peace that You want for me. Enable me to undercut my self-serving agendas, repeal my fears, capsize my contrived wisdom, and annul my vagrant philosophies.

And teach me to rebel against that which has rebelled against You, for in these things I find Your peace.

I pray all of this in Jesus's Name. Amen.

A Thought to Carry with Me Today
"You can't even have pieces of peace
Unless you have all of God."
~ Craig D. Lounsbrough

Before this day, I release to God...

_____

_____

_____

_____

Evening Prayer

Dear God:
I want to sleep in peace, just like I want to live in peace. My dreams are not peaceful. In fact, they're anything but. They're dark sometimes. They're frightening at other times. They leave me feeling weighed down with a darkness that takes me hours to shake.

And so, I pray that the peace that I am seeking from You will grant me a peace in my sleep that calms my nights and lends serenity to my dreams. Grant me a peace that I am never without, whether I'm awake or asleep. Gift me with a peace that is untouched by

234

whatever the world is going to throw at me. Help me to walk in the storms of life with a calm that I probably won't understand, but a calm that is more real than the force of any storm.

Give the me "peace that passes all understanding." Your peace. A peace that is superior to everything in our world that would seek to destroy it. A peace that's above anything that I will ever encounter. Dear God, this is the peace for which I pray tonight.

I pray all of this in Jesus' Name. Amen.

A Thought to Prepare for Tomorrow
"We're desperate for peace because it comes to
us so rarely, and when it does, it seems to evaporate
at the very moment that it draws near us. But that is
peace based on circumstances that are as fleeting as
the peace that comes with them, where the peace
that comes with God makes everything else
flee that draws near it."
~ Craig D. Lounsbrough

From this day, I release to God...

_____

_____

_____

_____

_____

Conclusion

Too many times we have been stolen. Whether we gave the world permission to carry out the heist, or we did it ourselves. However it happened, too many times we've been stolen.

But the real thievery rests in the belief that we've not been stolen at all. We borrow, manufacture, or fictionalize an identity that leads us to believe that who we are was never absconded with at all. We quantify any struggles or misgivings about ourselves as that treacherous and often tumultuous journey of self-actualization.

Yet, something is missing. There is a lapse of legitimacy to it all. An absence of authenticity. Some sort of thin shallowness and aching superficiality. We've dressed in the finery of that which we believe will be appealing to others, or we find ourselves clothed in the rags assigned to us by those who dare to categorize us for their self-serving convenience. Yet, it remains an unsettling fictional rendition that seeks to betray the authentic self that it can never articulate or mimic.

Too many of us live and eventually die living out a false self. We exhaust this existence never discovering the immensity of who God created us to be. That marvelous essence never flourishes because it was held hostage to the fictional and fabricated. This devotional was written to bring a halt to such tragedies. To rip the false self away and breathe life into the true self. For to die never having lived is the most devastating (but likewise most preposterous) death imaginable.

It is my hope that you have finally begun to live, and that you will never cease such an incredible journey as you embrace God's genius manifest in you. Over the next thirty-one days I would encourage you to hold these thirty-one truths up against everything that you are not. It is my hope that they declare the authenticity of your true self with such force that all that is false within you dies the death of their own lies.

Here is who and what God says you are. Here is your true self ready to become your truth.

Thirty-One I Am's

1. I am adopted into God's Family (Ephesians 1:5, Romans 8:14-19, Galatians 4:5-7, Psalm 27:10)
2. I am a child to the King of Kings (1 Peter 2:9, Galatians 4:5-7, John 1:12, Romans 8:14-19)
3. I am passionately loved (Romans 8:38, Psalm 56:8, Isaiah 43:4)
4. I am a new person in Christ (2 Corinthians 5:17, Isaiah 43:18-19)
5. I am not weary (Galatians 6:9, 2 Thessalonians 3:13, Matthew 11:28, Psalm 94: 19)
6. I can do all things through Christ (Philippians 4:13, Deuteronomy 20:4, 1 Corinthians 15:57)
7. I am remarkably made (Psalm 139:14, Psalm 139:1-24, Genesis 1:27)
8. I am extraordinary (Ephesians 2:10, Genesis 1:27)

9. I am provided for (Matthew 6:30-35, 2 Peter 1:3, Deuteronomy 20:4)
10. I am valuable (1 Peter 1:18-19, John 3:16, Psalm 56:8)
11. I am chosen (John 15:16, 1 Peter 2:9, Ephesians 1: 4)
12. I am courageous (Deuteronomy 31:6, 2 Timothy 1:7)
13. I am a conqueror (Romans 8:37, Deuteronomy 20:4, 1 Corinthians 15:57)
14. I am strong (Deuteronomy 31:6, Psalm 138:3, Isaiah 40:30-31, 2 Corinthians 12: 10)
15. I am forgiven (1 John 1:9, Ephesians 1:7, Colossians 3:13)
16. I am blameless (Ephesians 1:4, 2 Corinthians 5:17)
17. I am fearless (2 Timothy 1:7, Psalm 23: 4, Psalm 56:3-4)
18. I am blessed (Ephesians 1:3, Matthew 5:1-48, 3 John 1:2)
19. I am righteous (Romains 1:5, 2 Corinthians 5:21)
20. I am pure (1 John 3:3,1 Peter 1:22)
21. I am patient (1 Corinthians 13:4, Galatians 6:9)
22. I am kind (Colossians 3:12, 1 Corinthians 13:4-5)
23. I am covered in God's armor (Ephesians 6:10-18, Psalm 18:2)
24. I am wrapped in God's arms (some translations say wings) (Psalm 91:4 TPT, Isaiah 25:4)
25. I am heard (Psalm 116:1-2, 1 John 3:22)
26. I am enough (2 Peter 1:3, 2 Corinthian 3:5, Colossians 2:10)

27. I am not alone (Deuteronomy 31:6, Isaiah 54:10, Psalm 48:14, Psalm 46: 1-2)
28. I am healed (1 Peter 2:24, Isaiah 53:5, Psalm 147:3)
29. I am accepted (Romans 15:7, Romans 8:14-19, Romans 8:34, Ephesians 1:3-6, Colossians 1:21-22)
30. I have a future (Jeremiah 29:11, Romans 8:28, Philippians 1:6)
31. I am at peace (Philippians 4:6-7, Psalm 23, Mathew 6, Psalm 94: 19)

These are not opinions. They are facts that are as eternal as the God Who stated them. They are not the things that God would say to sooth a crushed self-image. They are the essence of your being and the foundation of your design. These are the truths that define what the world cannot. They are the genius of God woven into the genius of your design as He brought unparalleled majesty, unbridled originality, and unrelenting creativity to bear in creating you. These are you. And I would beg you not to compromise the least part of who and what God rigorously built into you. Being who God made you to be is 'being' in the greatest sense imaginable.

Craig D. Lounsbrough

Appendix

Resources to Maximize Your Prayer Life

Structuring an Effective Prayer Life – My Own Personal Strategies

"I think that one of the greatest prayers to pray is to ask for sufficient wisdom to pray the right prayers".
~ *Craig D. Lounsbrough*

Prayer is intentional. So is our preparation for it. We would be wise to invest time and energy in structuring our lives in a manner that both sustains and perpetuates a bold and thoughtful prayer life.

Over the years, these are several of the things that I have found helpful in achieving those exact goals. I would suggest that you build them into your prayer life.

Have a Designated Place to Pray
Find that place in your house or apartment that becomes the place where you meet God. When you do this, this place takes on an aura or a sense that this is where you encounter God. This is where both of you meet up. The feeling that this is the place where you meet God can enhance your prayer time, add vitality to it, and make it easier to be consistent.

Have a Designated Time to Pray
While we are to pray throughout the day, find one time that is exclusively your time with God. Once you find

it, protect it. While mornings tend to be busy for most people, try to find a time at the beginning of your day as you are more rested during that time. In addition, the act of prayer sets a balanced and energized tone for your day that nothing else can set in such a potent and sustaining manner.

Distractions
Unless your house is on fire or somebody's dying, things can wait. We have this pressing sense that we've got to get things done and check them off of our list. There's something critical about doing that. Otherwise, we'll be dwelling on everything that we need to do once we're done praying instead of focusing on the fact that we're praying. And in taking time with God we have set the stage for God to step in and take care of everything on our list in ways that are far more efficient and thorough than we could have imagined.

Track Scriptures in Your Bible As God Gives Them to You
Have a Bible where you can track scriptures that God brings to you, or ones that you discover throughout the day, or ones that a friend gives you. Underline them in your Bible, place the date by them, and mark the page with a sticky note. Begin to build a journal that outlines your prayer journey, thereby giving your prayer life a multi-dimensional sense that extends beyond this single moment of prayer.

Have Some Accompanying Material
Have something that you read daily or possibly weekly as part of your prayer time. This could be a pamphlet,

a regular devotional, a newsletter, an article that you found of value, a chapter in a book, etc. Have these to refer to as part of your time with God to deepen and broaden the experience.

Your State of Mind
Realize that some days you might come to prayer very focused. Other days, you might be far more scattered. Some days you might have a strong sense of what you want to pray about, and at other times you may not. Simply bring who you are at that moment. It's not so much what you showed up with, it's the fact that you showed up.

To End Your Day
Have some Bible reading at the end of your day to round out your day. This could be a devotional, or part of reading through a particular book of the Bible, a "One Year Bible," or referencing a scripture that you read during your time in the morning. Bring a close to your day that helps to settle the demands that you experienced that day.

Conclusion
I would encourage you to diligently include these disciplines in your prayer life. They will add a depth and degree of enrichment that will enhance your prayer life in ways that can and will be transformational.

Obstacles to Prayer - My Own Personal Observations

*"I want to live a life where prayer is the first thing
that I do, the second thing, the third thing, and the last
thing after the prayer has been answered."*
~ Craig D. Lounsbrough

Many of the obstacles to prayer are things that we have
not given sufficient attention to or presume as
somehow normal, appropriate, or of no real concern.
They are the things that cleverly present themselves as
rather casual issues that are of little importance. In our
largely contrived busyness, we have hastily
underestimated their importance and have assigned
them to some place of irrelevance until we can get to
them (which we rarely do). Therefore, seated all around
us are destructive factors that lay hidden in the fields of
our ignorance.

These things represent a less than disciplined
understanding as to how God has called us to live out
our lives. Yet, despite the fact that we have sidelined
these destructive factors, they have sufficient potency
and ample power to block our prayers. As such, we
should not live unawares of such subtle power sitting
hidden all around us. Rather, we should set out on a
hunt for them, rigorously ferret them out, and then
exorcise them out of our lives.

We have outlined a handful of these destructive factors
that too often lay hidden in our lives. And in wondering
how or why our prayer lives seem so ineffectual, we

might ask if any of these factors have found a place of residence in our lives.

Obstacles to Prayer

Sin. Sin is an intentional living outside of the will of God that places us at odds with who God created us to be. Sin is described as "anything that separates us from God." If we are engaging in such behaviors, we come to prayer separated from the God to Whom we are praying.

Self-Centered Agendas. We tend to live out our lives based on our agendas and our perception of what is in our best interest. Therefore, we do not come to prayer seeking God's direction, will, insights, and perspective. Rather, we come with a prepared agenda where we wrangle with God in order to achieve these agendas or obtain the resources to achieve them.

Distractions. Prayer becomes the thing that we squeeze into the many demands in our lives. It's something that sits somewhere near the bottom of the rather extensive checklist that outlines our obligations and duties. We intend to give prayer space and time, but it often falls prey to the many other demands that press prayer off of our calendar.

Our Perspective of Prayer. Often, we have developed an understanding of prayer as something that has value, but something that can be missed without extensive consequence to our lives. We don't see it as interacting with the God of the universe as an integral part of growing in relationship with Him and profoundly living out our lives in that relationship. It is more a prescribed duty that (if fulfilled) is optimal. But should time not permit, there is little lost in the absence of it.

Shiny Object and Squirrels. There are many things that vie for our attention, and we give many of those things that very attention. In reality, most of those things are not imperative to life and living, although we grant them that exact status. It is often assumed that if something in our life demands our attention it is because ignoring it will have dire consequences, when in fact deferring the majority of these things is unlikely to result in any consequence of consequence. Therefore, we rank these things as to their perceived importance as well as the pressing nature of whatever they might be demanding of us. As such, in the perpetual bombardment of a busy life, prayer is easily set aside.

Lack of Faith. We are lacking in faith. Prayer is understood within the context of the faith with which we use it. The lack of faith either inhibits our prayers as we feel that we bring very little to the process, or we bring little to the process because we don't necessarily believe in it. We forget that coming to prayer regardless of our level of faith is in itself the exhibition of faith. We must remember that the size of our faith only becomes an issue when we refuse to use the faith that we have.

Unmet Expectations. We come to prayer with expectations regarding the outcome of our prayers, or what we wish to obtain by praying. If those outcomes are not achieved (in light of the greater outcomes that God has for us), we feel that prayer is ineffectual or irrelevant. If it fails to generate our prescribed outcomes we are quick to label it as irrelevant or entirely powerless. Our assumptions rest in the belief that our expectations are the ones that are right for our situation, rather than being the one's that we should explore in order to determine what might actually be right for us.

A Jaded Heart. God has not answered our prayers in the way that we wanted, or in the time frame that we wanted, or maybe He didn't answer them at all (which is an answer, but not the one that we hoped for). We have found God disappointing, demanding, a less than generous God, and one that crushes our desires despite how passionately we bring them to Him. We refuse to understand that God cannot fulfill many of our desires because it is the fulfilling that would do the crushing. Therefore, we either refuse to pray any longer, or we do so in such a limited fashion that it can barely be defined as prayer.

The Lure of the World. The world is chock full of enticing things that have no depth and lack any substance whatsoever. And therein lies the absurdity of it all. In some breathless fashion we chase after that which we believe will do the things that we're chasing them to do. And once we actually catch them (or in some cases realize that we can't because nobody does), we're struck with the chafing reality that these things weren't what they appeared to be, or they didn't possess the resources that we had errantly endowed them with. But without missing a beat, we immediately set out to chase the next thing for the exact same reasons. And prayer goes wanting.

The Insurance Policy. Is prayer some supplemental thing that we do out of guilt, or a sense of obligation, or to cover the holes that we might have left in our efforts to tidy up our lives? Is prayer the means by which we ensure that our efforts are pushed through to our satisfaction in case we didn't push quite hard enough? Is prayer that safety net that we keep in place just in case the world fails us, or we fail ourselves? Is prayer that supplemental insurance policy that we hold onto 'just in case?' Prayer is not insurance. Rather, it's the assurance that we won't need insurance.

Conclusion
There are many things that create obstacles to our prayer. And maybe one of the biggest is our unwillingness to look for them. Either way, we would be wise to thoughtfully inventory our lives and ferret out anything that would create and sustain any such obstacle regardless of what it might be. Take careful inventory of the things that create obstacles for you and be intentional in your removal of them.

www.ingramcontent.com/pod-product-compliance
Lightning Source LLC
Chambersburg PA
CBHW061724120626
46550CB00005B/1701